David Baker

THE
ORGAN

A brief guide to its construction,
history, usage and music

Shire Publications Ltd

Cover: *The organ of Wymondham Abbey, Norfolk.*

Printed in Great Britain by CIT Printing Services, Press Buildings, Merlins Bridge, Haverfordwest, Dyfed SA61 1XF.

British Library cataloguing in Publication Data: Baker, David, 1952 —. The Organ. I. Title. 786.5190902. ISBN 0-7478-0131-2.

Contents

1. How an organ works 5
2. History and types 19
3. Technique and repertoire 59
4. Gazetteer 77
5. Further reading 87
6. Discography 89
   Index 95

Acknowledgements

I am very grateful to a number of people who have helped in the preparation of this book. Tony Freeman-Cosh, of Picture Perfect Photography, Wymondham, Norfolk, spent much time producing photographs of the outside and the inside of the organs of Wymondham Abbey. Joan Welsby carried out the research and clerical work associated with locating and obtaining permission to use the other illustrations and compiling the discography. Christine Christopher typed the early manuscript drafts. To them all I give my thanks.

Pictures are acknowledged as follows: Bildarchiv Foto Marburg, Frankfurt, page 30; Birmingham City Council, page 46; Cheshire Life Magazine, courtesy of Charles Legh, page 35; Peter Collins, Leicester page 57; Cox Knuf-Jongman at Frits Knuf BV Buren, page 17; English Heritage, page 54 (left); Cadbury Lamb, page 37; Landesinstitut für Pädagogik und Medien, Dudweiler, page 20; Daniel Malnati, Waltzing-Arlon, Belgium, pages 24, 28, 32, 33, 94; Noel Mander and Company Limited, pages 4, 21, 36, 39, 50, 54 (right), 56, 82, 88; National Gallery of Scotland, by gracious permission of HM the Queen, page 18; Picture Perfect, Wymondham, cover and pages 6 (lower), 9, 10, 12, 15, 38; Praetorius, *Syntagma Musicum II*, pages 6, 22, 23, 25, 26; Priory Records, pages 29, 31, 55; Rijksdienst voor Monumentenzorg, Zeist, Holland, page 27; Thursford Collection, Norfolk, page 52; Ian Tracey, page 8; J. W. Walker and Sons Limited, pages 40, 41, 42, 43, 44, 45, 48, 58, 84. The musical examples on pages 63, 66, 67, 68, 70, 72, 74 and 75 are by Joan Welsby and the drawings on page 7 by Rachel Lewis.

The Organ

The organ of Magdalen College, Oxford, a two-manual organ by Noel Mander. The Great organ is in the 'chair' position, in a stone case on the chapel screen.

1
How an organ works

What is an organ? Sir Christopher Wren, architect of St Paul's Cathedral, London, described the instrument as a 'kist of whistles'. He was being uncomplimentary (he disagreed violently with the man who was building the organ for the cathedral), but his description was basically correct. The pipe organ is little more than a box of 'whistles' activated by one or more keyboards (similar to those found on pianos or harpsichords) and supplied with air from a bellows (like those used to help light a fire).

The pipes

A basic organ pipe, a *flue pipe*, makes its sound in much the same way as does the orchestral flute, in which the player's lungs are the bellows and provide the air. The air passes from his or her mouth (the equivalent of the organ's windchest) and across the mouth of the flute. As the air is split within the flute or the organ pipe, it vibrates and creates sound. The sound is then magnified through the rest of the instrument or pipe. Putting fingers over the holes on the flute makes the instrument (and the column of air within it) longer and so the sound is lower in pitch. Organ pipes are the same: the longer they are, the lower the note.

Some organ pipes, *reed pipes*, make sound in a different way. The principle is as before: air passes into the pipe through its base (called the foot) and a

vibration is set up, causing a sound. Here, though, the vibration is caused by a reed fixed inside the foot or boot of the pipe. Several instruments of the orchestra make their sound in the same way, for example the oboe or the bassoon. Indeed, some of the stops on an organ are called after instruments of the orchestra.

The length of a pipe affects the pitch of the note produced and in an organ of average size the pipes vary in length from a few inches to 16 feet (4.9 metres). In larger instruments the biggest pipes may be 32 feet (9.8 metres) or more long.

Reed pipes sound different from flue pipes, in the way that an orchestral flute sounds different from an oboe. The shape of the organ pipe itself can alter the quality or timbre of the sound produced. The basic sound which an organ makes comes from the *principal* pipes. These are flue pipes with a simple cylinder above the pipe mouth. They make hard bright notes. If a stopper is placed in the top of the pipe, a much softer, fluty sound is produced, and the sound is twice as deep in pitch as that of an open pipe because the column of air is twice as long.

There are many other shapes of organ pipe, each of which alters the sound in some way. Some pipes are conical; others are stopped but with an open chimney sticking out of the top of the stopper; some are square; some are triangular; others are twice the length which they

The Organ

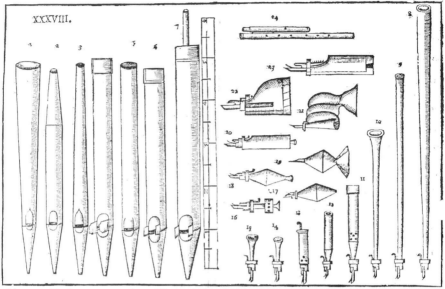

Above: *Various organ pipes, illustrated in Michael Praetorius, 'Syntagma Musicum II: De Organographia Parts I and II'. Note the different pipe lengths and shapes. Those on the right-hand side of the print are reed pipes.*

Left: The author sitting amongst the pipes of the organ of Wymondham Abbey, Norfolk.

need to be, but with a hole in the middle; a few have a flat shape like a saucer on top. Most organ pipes are made of metal — usually an alloy of some kind (zinc, tin and lead are metals commonly used), though pipes are also made of wood. Wooden pipes are often stopped and usually produce a mellower sound than metal ones. Very occasionally other materials have been used, for example bamboo.

Metal flue pipes are tuned by lengthening the pipe to lower or flatten the pitch and by shortening it to raise or sharpen the pitch. This is usually done by means of a tuning slide, a cylinder of metal which fits around the top of the pipe and which can be moved up or down to lengthen or shorten the pipe as required. In older organs, flue pipes were tuned by opening out the top of the pipe and broadening the diameter to sharpen the pitch or narrowing the pipe to flatten it. This was done by means of a tuning cone, a cone-shaped tool whose narrow end was inserted into the pipe to open it up and sharpen it or whose hollow broad end was put over the top of the pipe to narrow and flatten it. The tuning cone would be driven into the pipe using a hammer. This tended to damage the pipes over a period of time, hence the use of tuning slides. Some pipes, especially those in case-fronts, are tuned by peeling away a strip of metal at the top of the pipe and hence shortening or (if the metal is rolled back up) lengthening the pipe. Stopped flue pipes are tuned by adjusting the stopper up or

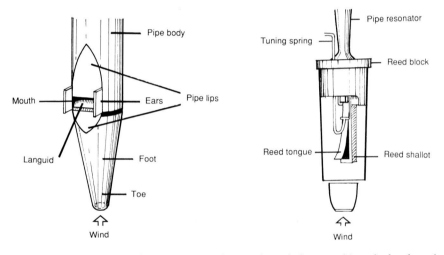

Left: *A typical flue pipe. In flue pipes the wind enters through the toe and into the foot from the windchest on which the pipe is sitting. The toe fits into a hole in the windchest and the foot is usually supported upright by a wooden rack. The wind travels up through the foot to the mouth, where it is forced through a narrow passage between the languid, which blocks off all but the very front of the pipe, and the pipe mouth itself. This causes the column of air to vibrate and make a sound. The sound comes out through the mouth and, if the pipe is open at the top, through there as well. The languid may be nicked by the organ-pipe voicer in order to alter the way in which the pipe 'speaks'. The pipe body will vary in length depending upon the pitch of the note and whether it is an open or a stopped pipe, and its shape on the kind of register (principal, flute, et cetera).*

Right: *A typical reed pipe. Wind enters the pipe through the foot, as in a flue pipe. Inside the foot of the pipe is the reed shallot against which the reed tongue vibrates when the air enters. The reed tongue and shallot are mounted on the reed block, on which is also mounted the pipe resonator. The tuning spring is linked to the tongue and allows the organ tuner to alter the length of the reed tongue and so change its pitch. The length of the resonator will vary according to the pitch of the pipe and the type of register. Reed pipes are usually made of metal, though the resonators, especially in larger pipes, are also made of wood. Altering the length of the resonator also changes the pitch.*

The Organ

The choir console of the organ of Liverpool Anglican Cathedral, 1960.

2.5 inches (3.8 to 6.4 cm). On larger organs, and especially those built in the latter part of the nineteenth and the first half of the twentieth century, wind pressures are often considerably higher. One of the reed stops of the organ at Liverpool Anglican Cathedral is on 50 inches (127 cm) pressure.

The mechanism

So that the organ can make a sound, air has to reach the pipes. The bellows supply the air. Before the advent of electricity, organs had to be hand-blown. In some old country churches it is still possible to see the pumping lever which fills the bellows with air. Other ways of providing the wind included men standing on the bellows or in treadmills. It is thought that some ancient organs used water to provide air to the pipes (see chapter 2). More recently hydraulic and gas engines have been used to fill the bellows, though most organs are now supplied with air by an electric blower.

From the bellows the air is supplied to the windchest by means of trunking. The windchest is a wooden box with holes on top into which the pipes fit. Pipes of the same type are grouped together in *ranks*. Sometimes the pipes are arranged in order of size, with the largest ones at the left-hand or bass end of the windchest. Often, however, the pipes are placed on the chest so that the largest pipes are either all in the middle or at either end. This prevents the big pipes from drawing the wind to one end of the chest.

The instrument is played from one or more keyboards. Those played by the hands are usually called manuals (*manus*

down within the pipe. Reed pipes are tuned by adjusting the length of the reed in order to make it vibrate more rapidly (producing a higher note) or more slowly (producing a lower note) or by changing the length or shape of the resonator. The organ builder can alter the way in which the pipes *speak* (that is, sound) by varying the basic dimensions or *scaling* of the pipe or by altering the way in which it is *voiced*. For instance, nicks in the piece of metal against which the air is forced to pass in a flue pipe (the *languid*) can alter the quality of the sound and the speed at which it is produced. The timbre and volume can also be altered by the pressure of the air entering the pipe. The wind pressure is measured by the extent to which the air coming from the bellows can move a water or similar gauge. On smaller or older instruments, pressure is typically 1.5 to

How an organ works

is the Latin word for hand). The larger pipes are played from a special keyboard designed to be used by the organist's feet. The pedals normally control the bigger pipes.

The keyboards are linked to the windchest and hence the pipes by the action or key mechanism. Several different kinds of action exist. The oldest and most durable is known as *tracker* or *mechanical* action. Here, the keys are linked by a series of trackers (thin trace rods, usually made of wood) to pallets underneath the windchest. When a key is depressed, the pallet is activated and allows wind into the pipes immediately above it. Because the windchest is bigger than the keyboard and in many cases the pipes are not arranged in the same order as the keys, the tracker action incorporates a *roller board*, which ensures

that the keys allow the correct pipes to sound, even if they are not situated above that part of the keyboard to which they relate. The most extreme example of this matching is the bottom C sharp key, which on many organs will have its pipes at the top (right-hand) end of the windchest — as far away as they can be from the key.

Some organs have tubular-pneumatic, electro-pneumatic or electric action. In a *tubular-pneumatic* action the trackers are replaced by small tubes which link the keys to the pallet. When a key is depressed, a puff of air travels through the tube and activates a pneumatic motor which opens the pallet and allows wind into the pipes above. In an *electro-pneumatic* action the tube is replaced by electric wiring. Depressing the key completes an electric circuit, which in turn

Left: *The organ bellows and tracker action of the Wymondham Abbey organ.*
Right: *The electric action of the Wymondham Abbey organ.*

The James Davis one-manual chamber organ of 1810 at Wymondham Abbey.

a need to have the keyboards separated from the pipes, then tracker action is often not feasible. Wherever possible, most organ builders now prefer to build traditional mechanical actions.

The layout and tonal design

The variety of sound in an organ comes from ranks of pipes not only of different pitches but of different shapes and in different locations too. The ranks of pipes can usually be played separately or in combination, except in the case of the higher-pitched ranks, which are often grouped together. Because these pipes are very small even in the lowest part of their compass, the ranks consist of the same size of pipe further up the scale so that they do not become too small to be made and to sound effectively. These groups of ranks are known as *mixture* stops.

The organist sits at a *console*, where there are the keyboards and the pedals. On either side of the console are the stopknobs which control the ranks of pipes. If the organist sits down at the console, switches on the organ blower and then plays a chord on one of the manuals, nothing will happen unless one or more of the stops is pulled out. Beneath each rank or group of ranks of pipes on the windchest is a mechanism which stops wind from entering the pipes unless the player wishes the pipes to sound. In organs with tracker action, the mechanism is usually called a *slider*. In the 'on' position, the holes in the slider match with those in the windchest and allow the air through to the pipes; in the

activates the pneumatic motor. In an *electric* action the pallet is operated by a magnet (brought into use by completion of the electrical circuit as the key is depressed) instead of a pneumatic motor.

There are other types of action and windchest, though the basic principles remain the same. Tracker action allows the player to be in close contact with the instrument and the pipes. A much more sensitive touch can be used with such an action and a good player can articulate the sound of the pipes by the way in which he or she depresses the key. Tubular-pneumatic and electric actions are less sensitive, since there is no real contact between the player's fingers and the pallets. However, in very large instruments, or in locations where there is

How an organ works

'off' position, the slider holes do not match with those in the windchest and the air cannot enter the pipes. There are other mechanisms for shutting off the wind supply, but the basic principle is the same as with the slider. Choosing the most appropriate combination of stops is part of the organist's art and is discussed in chapter 3.

The manuals and pedals each control different sets of ranks on one or more windchests. Large instruments can have as many as four or five manuals and over one hundred stops. Most instruments have two or three manuals and pedals and between twenty and forty stops. Some instruments — usually called *chamber organs* — have only one manual and no pedals.

The groups of pipe ranks controlled by each manual or the pedals are usually called *divisions*, though sometimes they are called 'organs', recalling the time when several different instruments were combined into one larger one. Each division has its own windchest and a different name. *Pedal* is an obvious one; the names of the other divisions require explanation, however. The *Great* division (or organ) is so called because it contains the main set of principal stops (usually called a chorus) and sounds grand and imposing. The *Swell* manual controls a division which is enclosed in a box with a set of shutters (usually looking like a Venetian blind) at the front. These shutters are operated by a *swell pedal* at the organist's feet. As they open, the sound gets louder or 'swells'. The *swell box* and its shutters enable the player to crescendo and diminuendo.

Most organs in Britain have Great, Swell and Pedal divisions. If there is a third manual it usually controls the *Choir* division. It was often thought that this term originated because the stops on this windchest were included in order to accompany choral music. However, the word 'choir' is a corruption of the word 'chair'. In older British and continental organs (as well as some recent instruments) part of the instrument is placed in a separate section behind where the player sits, hence the term *Chair* organ (the pipes are behind the organist's chair).

Some organs have a fourth manual which controls a variety of stops. In many instruments the division is called the *Solo* division, because the pipes are specially designed and voiced for playing melodic lines rather than full chords. The stops vary considerably both in timbre and power. Fourth (or fifth) manuals may also be labelled *Bombarde* or *Echo*. Bombarde divisions are made up of very powerful stops, as the name implies. An Echo section, on the other hand, consists of soft and delicate stops (usually in a swell box and perhaps placed some distance away from the main instrument) which can be used to echo the stops and sounds on the other, louder divisions.

In order to increase the power of the instrument, as well as to vary the sounds which can be produced, the manuals can usually be coupled together so that from one keyboard the pipes of two or more divisions can be made to sound at the same time. In mechanical-action instruments manuals are not all coupled together for long periods — especially if the touch is heavy — though larger

The Organ

tracker organs have electric or pneumatic coupling assistance mechanisms. In organs with other actions couplers can be freely provided and used. In some cases, for instance, it is possible to couple one manual to another at a different octave, or to couple a manual to itself at different octaves, with the option of having the original pitch silenced through the use of the 'unison off' device.

From time to time the organist will wish to change the *registration*, the combination of stops which have been drawn. It would soon become boring to the listener if the same sound came out of the instrument all the time. Stops can be changed by hand, and with older instruments that is the only option. On the European mainland it has often been the practice to employ an assistant to change

The swell shutters of the Wymondham Abbey organ.

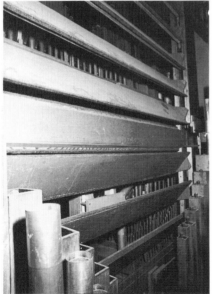

the stops for the organist, it being difficult for the player to pull out or push in the drawstops and play the music at the same time. In most modern instruments, however, registration aids are provided. These may be foot pedals or pistons which push out combinations of stops when depressed. On some instruments there are also thumb pistons — little buttons between the manuals which bring out different combinations of stops when pushed in. Registration aids are most common on organs with pneumatic, electric or electro-pneumatic action.

The physical layout of the organ varies considerably from location to location, country to country and era to era. Mechanical-action organs must be in one place and follow a simple and logical layout if they are to function effectively and with a light keyboard touch. Other actions allow pipes to be placed in different locations, and it is not unknown for divisions to be placed in completely separate parts of a building. In some large churches, for instance, the main organ is too far away from the congregation to be heard effectively and so a separate nave section is built in order to lead hymn singing. This has its own wind supply and is connected to the main instrument through an electric action.

Organs sound best when the pipes are enclosed at the back, sides and top by a case, usually made of wood. This focuses the sound and projects it into the building. An open location also ensures that the organ can easily be heard without the air being forced through the pipes. Unfortunately many organs, and especially those in churches, have been built without effective casing, or even with no casing at all, and in poor cramped locations.

The specification

The *specification* of an organ consists of a list of the stops, couplers and registration aids which the instrument possesses. The specification cannot tell how an instrument sounds, but it does give some indication of the range and nature of the various stops and the tone colours which they produce.

The large pipe organ of Wymondham Abbey, Norfolk (see cover), is well known for its fine sound and provides a typical example. The organ has three manuals and a Pedal division. Each division has a chorus of principal stops as its foundation.

The term *Open Diapason* is used in English organs to denote the basic principal stop in the organ. The term 'Diapason' comes from the Greek and approximates to the phrase 'of full compass'. The figures relate to the length, in feet, of the longest pipe of each rank. Thus the 4 foot Principal plays an octave higher than the 8 foot Diapason, and the Fifteenth two octaves higher. The Fifteenth is so called because it plays fifteen white notes (naturals) higher than the 8 foot stop; the Twelfth is twelve notes higher and the Seventeenth seventeen notes higher. The Twelfth and Seventeenth, and any other ranks whose longest pipe measurement includes a fraction (for example $1^1/3$, $1^3/5$, $2^2/3$), sound thirds and fifths away from the fundamental sound rather than octaves. They are called *mutation stops* because they change the basic pitch. For example, if the Twelfth stop is drawn on its own and the bottom C key is depressed, the note G $1^1/2$ octaves above is sounded.

As already noted, the very high-pitched ranks are grouped together as mixtures. The Roman numerals denote the number of ranks which are controlled by one stop and the figures show how far above the fundamental 8 foot pitch the pipes sound. Thus 19 = 19 notes, 22 = 22 notes, and so on. The III rank mixture is called 'sharp' because of the bright edgy tone which its high ranks add to the Great organ chorus. The higher-pitched stops are not normally played on their own, but in combination with 8, 4 and 2 foot pitch stops.

Each division has other kinds of ranks apart from the principals. The Great organ, for instance, has three flute stops, the Double Stopped Diapason, the Stopped Diapason and the Block Flute. The first two, as their names imply, are made up of stopped pipes. The Block Flute is an open rank, but with cone-shaped pipes. The division is completed by two reed stops, the Trumpet and the Clarion. These ranks can be played from both the Great and the Choir manuals. If played from the Choir keyboard, they can be accompanied on the Great manual, or *vice versa*. The Trumpet and Clarion are very loud stops, best used for solo purposes, for the pipes are mounted horizontally high up inside the case. Ranks located in this position are described as being *en chamade*, the French phrase for sounding a battle fanfare. At the other extreme is the Dulciana, probably the quietest rank on the organ. It has very small-scale pipes and is voiced as a very soft principal stop.

The Organ

The pipes of the Pedal division are twice the size of those on the manuals, for the most part; the 16 foot stops are the equivalent of the 8 foot stops on the manuals, for example. The higher-pitched Pedal stops can be used to play solos while the manuals provide the accompaniment. The Shawm (named after the predecessor of the orchestral oboe) is the best stop to use for this purpose. Its pungent reedy tone can be heard clearly above the accompaniment, played on the manuals. The Sackbut (the name for the medieval trombone) is the largest and one of the loudest stops on the organ. It adds a deep growling bass

The specification of the organ of Wymondham Abbey, Norfolk.

GREAT ORGAN
Double Stopped Diapason	16+
Open Diapason	8
Stopped Diapason	8
Dulciana	8
Principal	4
Block Flute	4
Twelfth	$2^2/3$
Fifteenth	2
Seventeenth	$1^3/5$
Mixture	19-22 II
Sharp Mixture	22-26-29 III
Trumpet	8
Clarion	4
Swell to Great	

SWELL ORGAN
Open Diapason	8
Hohlflute	8
Salicional	8
Voix Celeste (TC)	8
Principal	4
Fifteenth	2
Cornet	12-15-17 III
Mixture	19-22 II
Contra Hautboy	16
Trumpet	8
Basset Horn	8
Clarion	4
Tremulant	
Swell Octave	
Swell Suboctave	
Swell Unison Off	

CHOIR ORGAN
Chimney Flute	8
Viola da Gamba	8
Principal	4
Stopped Flute	4
Flageolet	2
Larigot	$1^1/3$
Cymbel	29-33-36 III
Trumpet	8*
Clarion	4*
Swell to Choir	

PEDAL ORGAN
Open Wood Bass	16
Contra Gamba	16
Bourdon	16+
Octave	8+
Gamba	8+
Gedackt	8+
Fifteenth	4+
Mixture	19-22 II
Sackbut	32
Ophicleide	16
Clarion	8*
Shawm	4
Swell to Pedal	
Great to Pedal	
Choir to Pedal	

6 adjustable thumb pistons to each manual.
6 adjustable toe pistons to Great/Pedal and Swell.
reversible thumb pistons to manual to Pedal couplers, Swell to Great coupler.
reversible toe pistons to Swell to Great and Great to Pedal couplers, 16 foot and 32 foot reed
    stops.
reversible thumb piston for Swell tremulant.

*   Denotes borrowed from Great Organ.
+   Denotes extended rank.

How an organ works

The organ console of Wymondham Abbey, a large three-manual organ by James Davis, 1793, rebuilt in 1954 and 1973.

to the louder combinations on the manual divisions.

The 16 foot Pedal Bourdon is one of the commonest organ stops and provides a gentle bass sound. The word comes from the French *bourdonner*, 'to buzz'. The word 'Gamba' is short for 'viola da gamba'; the organ stop is meant to imitate the instrument from which it takes its name. It has a firm cello-like sound. The Ophicleide is another powerful reed stop and sounds like the manual Trumpet ranks, except an octave lower. Like those of many of the stops on an organ, the name comes from an old orchestral instrument, in this case the predecessor of the bassoon. This use of the names of early instruments to de-

scribe organ stops shows how the main phase of organ development took place in the fifteenth, sixteenth and seventeenth centuries, when such orchestral instruments were prevalent and organ builders attempted to imitate them in their organs.

On organs with pneumatic, electric or electro-pneumatic actions, and exceptionally on mechanical-action instruments, it is possible to use the same set of pipes to make up different stops. As already noted, the Great Trumpet and Clarion can also be played from the Choir manual and (in the case of the Trumpet) the pedals because electric actions from the three divisions can activate these pipes. This technique of borrowing stops or pipes is often applied in modern organs. At Wymondham Abbey, for instance, the lower part of the Great Double Stopped Diapason provides the bass pipes for the Pedal Bourdon, while the Flute, the Gamba and the Fifteenth all share pipes with their 16 or 8 foot equivalent. Extending ranks in this way so that they form two or more stops of the same type at different pitches saves metal or wood, space and money. The principle of extension has been used throughout some organs, though in such cases the organ tone sounds thinner than it would if at least all the main ranks were independent of each other. Where space and funds are scarce, however, extension of ranks can help to provide a bigger Pedal division than would otherwise be the case.

The Swell stops can sound loud or soft because of their enclosure in the swell box. The Salicional (from the latin *salix*, 'willow reed') and Voix Celeste (French for 'celestial voice') are string stops. The pipes are small and narrow in scale and are voiced in such a way as to produce a sound similar to stringed instruments such as the violin and viola. The two ranks are slightly out of tune with each other in order to produce a beating effect similar to the vibrato on a violin. The Gamba stops on the Choir and Pedal divisions are also string stops. The Hohlflute is made of wood and has a hollow sound (the word *hohl* is German for 'hollow'). There are also principal stops on the Swell similar to those on the Great, including two mixtures. The Swell III rank mixture is labelled Cornet because the Seventeenth rank in its composition gives a brassy edge to the sound. The Swell division also contains four reed stops, all with names of orchestral instruments. When played together with the mixtures they produce a bright fiery sound. This is called the Full Swell effect. The Basset Horn is best used as a solo stop.

The Choir division is the smallest part of the organ. It has one Principal stop as the basis of the chorus and three flute stops. The 8 foot flute is made up of stopped metal pipes with little open chimneys in the tops of the stoppers. The 4 foot flute is made of stopped wooden pipes and the 2 foot Flageolet is made of open metal pipes. The Larigot is similarly constructed, being a high-pitched open flute stop. The Viola da Gamba is a string stop. The Cymbel is made of very small principal pipes and makes a bright tinkling sound.

All the stops are of full compass (that is, they operate throughout the keyboard or pedalboard) with the exception of the Voix Celeste, which stops at Tenor C (the C note which would be the lowest of the tenor voice's range). The specification shows which of the manuals can be coupled to each other and to the pedals. The Swell manual can be coupled to itself at the octave and sub-octave pitches, with the option of switching off the unison pitch at the same time. The Tremulant acts on the supply of wind to the Swell division and disturbs the flow so that the pipes sound as if they have a vibrato like the human voice or a stringed instrument. This device normally affects only the softer stops, and especially those which are most likely to be used for a solo.

The stop names do not say what materials the pipes are made of, with the exception of the large Open Wood stop on the Pedal division. In some organs more of the stop names include reference to their wood or metal construction. The Wymondham Abbey organ uses a combination of tracker action (the original mechanism of 1793), electro-pneumatic and electric actions (installed in 1954). Because the sliders are activated by electro-pneumatic action, it is possible to provide a number of registration aids. Thus there are six thumb pistons for each manual division and pedal, duplicated by toe pistons in the case of the Swell and Great divisions. When pressed, these pistons bring out various stop combinations, as determined by the organist. The pistons can be altered at will. Other pistons control particular stops or couplers, as noted on the specification. These pistons are all reversible. In other words, if the stop or coupler is not in use when the piston is pressed, it is activated. If it is in use, then pressing the piston withdraws the stop or coupler. The organ case is an imposing creation, complete with pinnacles and cherubs!

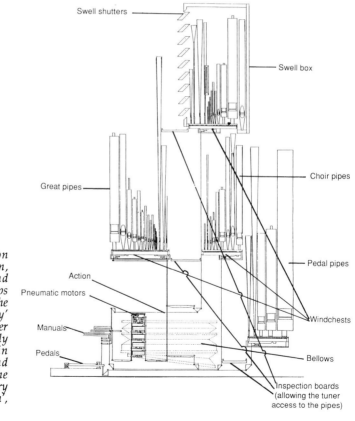

General section of an organ, showing sound boards and stops in profile, and the 'pneumatic key' movement (Barker lever). Originally published in Hopkins and Rimbault, 'The Organ: Its History and Construction', 1877.

Swell shutters

Swell box

Choir pipes

Great pipes

Pedal pipes

Action

Pneumatic motors

Windchests

Manuals

Pedals

Bellows

Inspection boards (allowing the tuner access to the pipes)

*A fifteenth-century positive organ from a painting of 1476 by Hugo van der Goes in the
National Gallery of Scotland.*

2
History and types

Early history

According to legend, the organ developed from the *syrinx* or Pan-pipes. The *syrinx* was essentially a rank of pipes of different lengths, each pipe playing one note when blown. The first record of such ranks of pipes being operated mechanically dates from *c.*250 BC, when a Greek engineer named Ktesibios is reputed to have invented the *hydraulos*. The *hydraulos* consisted of a simple rank of pipes activated from a crude keyboard and a wind supply controlled by water pressure. The instrument was often used at festivals to accompany celebrations.

Parts of a small Roman organ, dated to AD 228 and found at Aquincum, Hungary, have survived. The instrument appears to have had four ranks of pipes, one open and three stopped, of thirteen notes each, mounted on a wooden windchest with slides underneath to allow wind into the pipes. Nothing is known about how air was fed into the pipes of the Aquincum organ nor about the way in which the ranks were used.

However, it is known that by AD *c.*120 organs were being constructed with simple bellows to supply the wind. These instruments consisted of at most a few ranks and a series of sliders which were pushed in and out to control the pipes. In early medieval instruments, the sliders were connected to large keys which were pushed by the hand or

beaten with the fist. The organist was known as the *pulsator organorum* (beater of the organs).

Organs continued to be built after the fall of the western Roman Empire. In AD 757 the Byzantine emperor is said to have presented an organ to King Pepin of France. (Small organs were also made as royal gifts in subsequent centuries; Queen Elizabeth I presented an instrument to the Sultan of Turkey, for example.) It is unlikely that the instruments of the Eastern Roman Empire were used in churches; the Orthodox Church forbade use of the instrument. The organ was a secular instrument, as it had been in the earlier days of the Roman Empire, built to accompany a wide range of secular activities such as festivals, wedding feasts and gladiatorial contests.

Organs began to appear in churches from the tenth century onwards. It is not clear why this happened; perhaps the instrument's relative loudness or its association with public festivities made it seem appropriate to install organs in ecclesiastical buildings in order to enhance the services. Bishop Aldhelm wrote of the 'mighty voice' of the English organ in the seventh century AD. This power made the organ an attractive instrument for public gatherings, whether sacred or secular. The Benedictine order, for example, allowed the ringing of bells in church on festive occasions and the use of an organ at high points in festal services would also have enriched the worship considerably. The Benedictine order had a strong interest in music and several of its members were leading writers on the subject. It was in their churches and monasteries that organs first began to appear. In AD c.990 an organ was built for Winchester Cathedral (a Benedictine church) which was said to consist of four hundred pipes and 26 bellows. The instrument required two organists playing separate 'slider'

Hydraulis and cornu players; from a Roman mosaic of AD 230-40 at Nennig bei Trier, Germany.

The organ in Holywell Music Room, Oxford; built in 1790 by Donaldson of Newcastle, restored by Mander, 1985. Note that there are no pedals.

keyboards of twenty keys each.

Little is known about the exact size, nature or location of the medieval pipe organ and one can only conjecture as to the instrument's purpose. It would seem from surviving accounts of church services that the organ was used at the major festivals of the Christian year and may well have accompanied the singing of the choir or provided interludes in the plainsong. Early instruments were placed near the doors of churches, perhaps because they were used for fanfares on great occasions; later medieval organs seem to have been located near to the singers' stalls. The west end of the church did not become a standard location until the seventeenth century.

The organ keyboard grew more sophisticated as organ building became more

The Organ

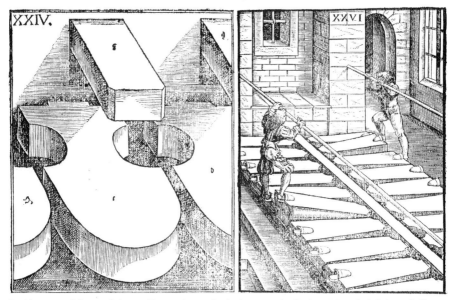

(Left) Manual keys of the Halberstadt Cathedral organ, built in 1361. (Right) Its bellows and calcants. Illustrated in Michael Praetorius, 'Syntagma Musicum II Parts I and II'.

widespread. A medieval composition for the organ in the Robertsbridge Codex (*c.*1325) requires a keyboard with a middle octave similar to that found on a modern instrument. The separation of ranks into stops was possible as a result of the invention of the windchest in the fourteenth century. Once wind could easily be admitted into separate channels, one each for all the pipes relating to every single note on the keyboard, then it was possible to introduce sliders into the top of the windchest placed at 90 degrees to those channels in order to stop off selected ranks when required.

Until then, most organs consisted of only one manual of limited compass and one large mixture stop, including 8 foot and possibly also lower ranks. Gradually the compass of the manual increased

and stop controls were introduced in order to allow ranks to be used separately from each other. Large church organs consisted mainly of multi-rank mixtures, with only a small number of 16, 8 and possibly 4 foot ranks controlled by stops. Variety was obtained by adding more manuals as much as by separating ranks on the same windchest. The organ built for Halberstadt Cathedral, Germany, in 1361, for example, had four keyboards, one being a series of levers activated by the knee, another a pedalboard played by the feet. The pipework of an organ such as that at Halberstadt would probably all have been open and made of metal.

It is not known when pedals first appeared. The first pedals may have been levers activated by the organist's knees;

they may not have controlled a windchest or pipes but merely pulled down the lower manual keys. Later medieval organs contained a small number of low-pitched stopped pipes placed in a separate case; such pipes may have been activated by pedals, thus providing a bass to the higher-pitched pipes played from the manual keyboards.

At the same time as large church organs such as that at Halberstadt were being built, smaller 'positive' and 'portative' organs were being developed. *Portative* organs, as the name implies, were carried by the player, who pumped the bellows with one hand while playing a small keyboard with the other. Portative organs consisted of two or three short-compass ranks of open metal pipes.

The *positive* organ, on the other hand, was placed on the floor of the church (as opposed to on a chancel screen or gallery). The bellows were activated by a second person, thus allowing the organist to use both hands to play the keyboard. Like the portative, the positive organ would have only a few ranks, but the compass would be fuller, and stopped bass pipes similar to those in larger organs also seem to have been included. Two positive organs built in the fourteenth century survive. The National Historical Museum in Stockholm houses the case of an organ built *c*.1390 and consisting of up to six ranks, played from a single manual and pedals. An organ reputed to be of similar age still survives in playable condition at the Church of Nôtre Dame de Valère in Sion, Switzerland, though the organ has been subsequently altered so much that it is impossible to tell which parts date from the fourteenth century and how the pipes originally sounded.

By *c*.1450 reed stops began to appear.

An old positive, illustrated in Michael Praetorius, 'Syntagma Musicum II: De Organographia Parts I and II'. Note the hand-operated bellows at the back of the instrument and the size of the pipes. The three small tabs at the side of the keyboard would have activated the sliders.

The Organ

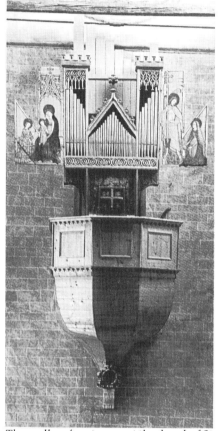

The swallows' nest organ at the church of St Valeria, Sion, Switzerland, c.1370. The pedal pipes were added in 1718 and the organ was restored in 1954.

A small portable organ known as the *regal* also dates from this time. The regal consisted of a keyboard which let wind into small reed pipes, often made of wood, blown by hand-operated bellows. The reed inside the pipe determined the pitch and not the pipe length, which altered only the timbre. As a result the instrument took up little space. Very small regal organs were built so that they could be folded into the shape of a Bible. Regal pipes were increasingly incorporated into larger pipe organs. It is not known why the regal organ was so called. It is unlikely that it had any royal connection but the name may be a corruption of the Latin *regula*, a reference to the instrument's regulating the pitch of the singers whom it would be used to accompany.

A treatise on instrument construction written by Henri Arnaut in the mid fifteenth century refers to the making of different kinds of reed pipe and gives details of organs then extant. In particular, he refers to the construction of chair organs or back positives. Similar in design to earlier positive organs, these organs would be placed behind the organist's back or chair so that he could easily turn to play the instrument as a contrast from the large organ. The chair or back positive was soon made playable from a keyboard situated above or below those which activated the main organ, and to which the chair keyboard could be coupled.

By the beginning of the sixteenth century organ builders were becoming increasingly inventive in their organ-pipe manufacture, no doubt because their clients were becoming more demanding. In continental Europe organs were seen as a symbol of civic wealth, and towns and cities vied with each other over the size and splendour of the instruments in their churches. Many early contracts for organs specify that the instrument has to be bigger and better than other organs in the area. Keen to obtain lucrative contracts, organ builders promised bigger and more powerful instruments with a greater variety of sounds than before. New kinds of pipe were introduced into organs in order to increase the range of tone colours available to the organist. Reed stops which imitated other instruments — Cornet, Trumpet, Crumhorn, Sackbut — proved especially popular. Mutation stops such as the Nazard, Tierce and Larigot, all designed to provide additional colour to solo stop combinations, also appeared. The Tremulant was invented; organs even acquired moving statuary and other special effects such as the Cymbelstern, a rotating star with a bell on the end of each point which jingled when the star moved.

In 1511 Arnolt Schlick, a Bohemian, produced the first published book on the organ, his *Mirror of Organ-builders and Organists (Spiegel der Orgelmacher und Organisten)*. He writes of organs which have a number of separate registers — principals, flutes, reeds, open and stopped pipes made of metal and of wood. The mechanism was little different from the modern tracker action and slider windchest. Schlick regarded the Pedal division as an extension of the main manual; indeed, in some organs the Pedal keyboard still activated stops placed on the windchest of the main division. However, it is clear from the music which Schlick himself wrote for the organ that the pedals would be expected to provide a full bass line to other parts played on the manual keyboards and a solo line accompanied by stops on the manuals, and to be capable of activating two, three and even four notes at the same time. This suggested that or-

ganists, at least in Germany, had to be capable of playing difficult pedal parts. Schlick also described the way in which organs were used in the church service. The instrument was to be used for the accompaniment of singers, the giving of notes to the priest intoning the service and the provision of musical interludes.

As the number of separable ranks on an organ increased, organists experimented with different ways of combining the stops to provide a wide variety of sounds. Chapter 3 discusses stop registration in detail. Surviving records of old organs and the way in which they were played show that only a small number of ranks would be combined at

Positive and Regal, illustrated in Michael Praetorius, 'Syntagma Musicum II: De Organographia Parts I and II'. Note the bellows and tuning implements. The 'pipes' of the regal can be seen immediately behind the keys. The instrument's size made it easily portable.

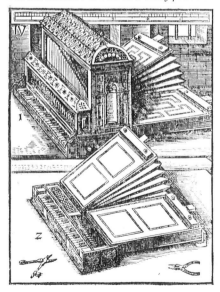

any one time. The amount of wind available to the organist on a hand-blown instrument would be limited. Only when mechanical blowing was introduced in the nineteenth century was it possible to combine a large number of stops together in the knowledge that there would be sufficient wind to enable all the ranks to sound properly. Organists in the sixteenth, seventeenth and eighteenth centuries concentrated on variety and subtlety in their stop registrations. Stop combinations on different divisions could also be contrasted with each other, while the Pedal division would include solo as well as chorus stops. The variety of sounds available to organists stimulated the composition of sets of variations on hymn tunes and plainchants, and in many of the north German and Dutch Protestant churches weekday organ recitals were regularly held from the sixteenth century onwards.

Three-manual and pedal organ, illustrated in Michael Praetorius, 'Syntagma Musicum II: De Organographia Parts I and II'. Note the Rückpositiv organ behind the console, the Pedal towers at either side of the console and the main part of the instrument.

Germany, Holland, Scandinavia: the Werkprinzip organ

By the end of the sixteenth century organs in Germany, Holland and Denmark were often very grand instruments. Three- and four-manual organs became increasingly common. The arrangement of the stops and the divisions was normally determined by the *Werkprinzip* (a modern German word meaning literally 'work-principle', but perhaps more meaningfully translated as 'division system').

The *Werkprinzip* organ developed from the simple chorus or *Blockwerk* organs of the late medieval period. As more chorus divisions were added, and as an increasing number of ranks were separated from the 'block', each division acquired a particular character and position within the instrument. Thus the *Hauptwerk* (main division) had the largest chorus, based on an 8 foot or a 16 foot principal stop and placed in the centre of the instrument. The *Rückpositiv* (back positive) was placed behind the player's seat at the front of the gallery and was

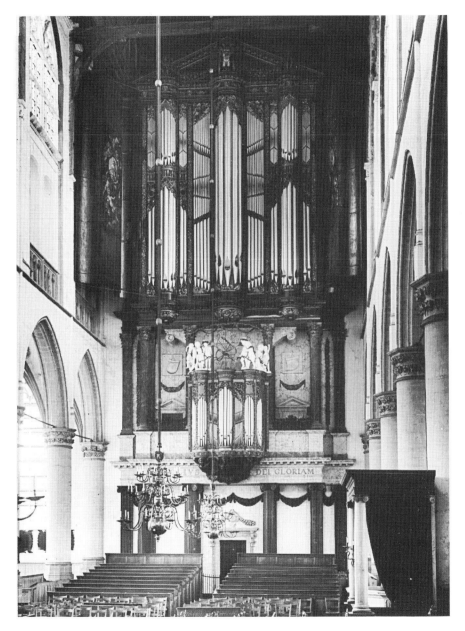

The organ of St Laurents, Alkmaar, Holland, 1638-45, rebuilt by Schnitger, 1723-6.

The Organ

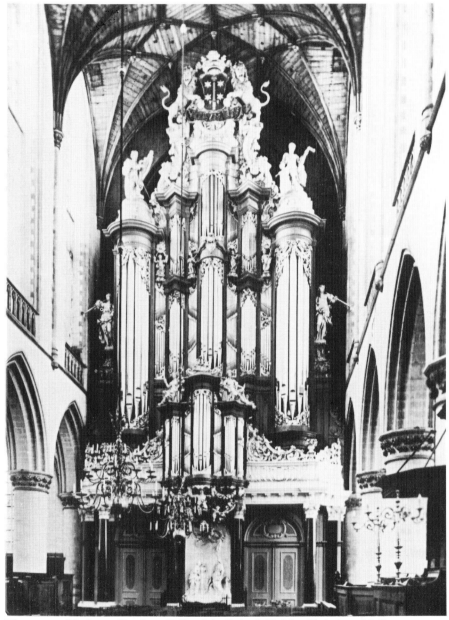

The organ of St Bavo, Haarlem, Holland, built in 1735-8 by Christiaan Müller.

based on a 4 foot or possibly an 8 foot principal stop. The *Rückpositiv* would contain higher-pitched stops and in general have a sharper sound, partly because of the kind of ranks which it contained and partly because of its position in relation to the rest of the instrument. The Pedal division would normally be divided between two large towers on either side of the Hauptwerk. Occasionally some or all of the ranks might be placed in or behind the main division.

Larger Werkprinzip organs contained other divisions. The *Oberwerk* (literally 'upperwork') was placed above the Hauptwerk. The *Brüstwerk* ('chestwork') was situated immediately above the console, almost facing the player's chest, hence the name. This division was usually the smallest in size, being based on a 2 foot principal and containing delicately voiced stops.

The large Werkprinzip organs of Germany, Holland and Denmark represent a peak in organ building which has rarely, if ever, been surpassed. Two of the finest organs of this kind are those of St Laurents, Alkmaar, and St Bavo, Haarlem, both in Holland.

The Alkmaar organ was rebuilt by F. C. Schnitger, a member of a famous family of seventeenth- and eighteenth-century organ builders, in 1723-6. The organ of St Bavo was built in 1735-8 by

The Silbermann organ in Freiberg Cathedral, Germany, built between 1710 and 1714.

The organ of the Benedictine abbey of Weingarten, Germany, built in 1737-50 by Joseph Gabler. Note the twin Rückpositiv cases.

Christiaan Müller. Both instruments are situated at the west end of large resonant churches. Each has three manuals (of which one controls a Rückpositiv) and a pedal. The two organs have a wealth of principal ranks, complete with several different mixtures, many different solo stops (both flue and reed) and a number of mutation ranks which can be used both in the chorus combinations and to provide solo tone colours. The Alkmaar organ has brilliant mixtures as the main characteristic of its sound. At St Bavo the power comes more from the full-scaled principal ranks, some of which have two sets of pipes. The cases of these organs are as grand as the instruments which they contain. The St Bavo case has lions,

harpists and a range of classical statues on the tops and sides of the casework.

The Werkprinzip organ was found throughout Germany, Austria, Holland, Scandinavia and Poland. There were variations in design and layout according to region or builder, though the basic principle of a series of divisions, each with its own particular position within the instrument, lasted well into the nineteenth century in all these countries. Such differences as there were related to the choice of divisions, the preference for 8 foot solo stops as opposed to mutation ranks, the style and composition (that is, the particular pitch of the ranks) of the mixtures, or the size and specification of the Pedal division.

The organ of Bordeaux Cathedral, France, built in 1748 by Bédos.

Thus for example in many later eighteenth-century continental organs the Rückpositiv division was omitted in favour of a second or third manual division either above or below the Hauptwerk. Some builders favoured lower-pitched mixtures and 8 and 4 foot solo flues and reeds (as opposed to the higher-pitched mixture and solo stops of the Schnitger organ). One of the most famous Germanic organ-building families of this period, the Silbermanns, adopted this approach. The organ of Freiberg Cathedral, Saxony, is perhaps the best known example of their work, being built by Gottfried Silbermann between 1710 and 1714. A very different instrument, but one still part of the Werkprinzip tradition, is the organ of the Benedictine abbey of Weingarten, Bavaria. Much depended on the type of location, the attitude of the builder and designer and the kind of music which was to be played on the instrument.

The classical organ of France

French organs developed differently from the sixteenth century onwards. While the two main divisions, *Grande Orgue* and *Positif*, were similar to the Germanic Hauptwerk and Rückpositiv in location and design, the instruments built in France were very different in voicing and approach. For example, the

The Organ

Pedal division was much smaller than in most German and Dutch instruments, only having two or three stops of (usually) 8 foot or 4 foot pitch. These stops were included primarily so that the organist could play the melody with his feet while the manual parts provided an accompaniment. German organs could also do this, though the Pedal divisions on these also provided both a bass to the manual divisions and an equal chorus to those of the other parts of the instrument.

The third and fourth manuals in French organs were usually an Echo organ, containing a full chorus, but only for the upper part of the instrument's compass, and of softer voicing, and a Récit division, also of short compass, and with only one or two stops — usually a Cornet and perhaps a reed rank. Larger French organs of the eighteenth century also occasionally had Bombarde divisions containing loud reed stops which could be coupled either to the main manual or the pedals.

By the middle of the seventeenth century French organs were designed according to certain basic principles, which were evident in all of the instruments constructed until the French Revolution put an end to organ building on any scale from 1790 until the 1840s. The principal choruses of the Grande Orgue and the Positif were based on a gently voiced stop, the Montre, so called because the bass pipes were shown in the case (*montrer* means 'to show'). The basic mixtures were called Fourniture because they 'furnished' the sound of the chorus, while the higher-pitched ones were called Cymbale.

Many of the solo effects on French or-

Ottobeuren, Germany: (left) the Trinity organ, c. 1761-6; (right) the 'Holy Ghost' organ, c. 1761.

The Epistle organ of Granada Cathedral, Spain, 1747.

gans came from the various mutation stops which they possessed. These would normally include a Cornet stop of four or five ranks on the Grande Orgue, consisting of 8 foot, 4 foot, $2^2/3$ foot, 2 foot and $1^3/5$ foot ranks. The Tierce rank, of $1^3/5$ foot pitch, gave the characteristic edge to the stop. In order to help the sound carry, the Cornet stop was often mounted on its own small windchest above the rest of the pipework, with wind conveyanced to it through metal tubes. The Mounted Cornet was also found in Germanic and English organs during the seventeenth and eighteenth centuries.

The Cornet stop on a French organ would often be combined with the reed stops on the Grande Orgue, along with the 4 foot principal, to produce a full brassy sound, called the *Grand Jeu*. The *Plein Jeu*, on the other hand, comprised the flue stops of the Grand Orgue and the Positif.

Stop registration on French organs of the seventeenth and eighteenth centuries was very stylised. A composer who marked the score with, for example, the words 'Grand Jeu', would know that the organist would understand that he had to draw certain stops and that the sound would be much the same, regardless of which instrument was being played. Solo stops or combinations of stops were indicated in much the same way. The phrase *'Tierce en taille'*, for example, meant that the Tierce rank (usually voiced as a flute rather than a principal stop) would be played with 8, 4, 2 and perhaps $1^1/3$ foot stops in the bottom half of its compass, accompanied on the Positif manual by 8 foot and possibly 4

foot flute stops. The conventions of French organ playing are discussed more fully in chapter 3.

Many French organs built before 1800 still survive, despite the French Revolution and an extensive rebuilding programme in the nineteenth century. The organ at Le Petit Andely, near Rouen in northern France, built in 1674 by Ingout, is a good example of the classical French organ, both in tonal design and appearance. Some eighteenth-century builders attempted to combine elements of the French and German instruments into one organ. The large four-manual organ built by Riepp at Ottobeuren Abbey, Bavaria, in 1761-6 combines German choruses with French solo stops, for example.

Organs in Spain, Portugal and Italy

Spanish and Portuguese organs developed in a different way from either French or Germanic instruments. While they had the same basic stoplists as the kind of organ already discussed, the emphasis was on powerful reed stops, often mounted horizontally (*en chamade*) at the front of the instrument. The Pedal division was usually less well developed than in German instruments and the third and fourth manuals controlled small divisions intended for echo or solo effects, as in French organs. Spanish and Portuguese church instruments were often placed in the arches on either side of what in an English church would be called the chancel (where the choir sits). There might well be an instrument on either side of the chancel area, and these instruments could be used antiphonally.

The organ at Adlington Hall, Cheshire, played by Handel in 1741 and 1751. It was possibly built by Bernhard Smith using older material.

It is now thought that the very first Swell divisions appeared in Spanish organs (not in English instruments, as originally thought) early in the eighteenth century. These swell organs were of short compass and contained only a few stops.

Italian organs from the sixteenth century to the nineteenth remained small, consisting normally of one manual with pedal pull-downs (that is, the pedals activated the lower keys of the manual rather than any independent pedal pipes). These instruments nevertheless included a wide range of stops — flue, reed, open, stopped — though until the eighteenth century the normal practice

The Organ

The organ of Pembroke College, Cambridge, a two-manual organ built by Noel Mander in 1980, based on early eighteenth-century pipework and case.

was to separate *all* the ranks on the windchest, even those of the highest pitch, which in other countries would form part of the mixture stops. This no doubt helped the organist to provide a wider range of sounds than would otherwise be possible from a small instrument. Registration was highly stylised, with different stops or combinations of stops being used to accompany each part of the Catholic mass, for which the Italian organ was primarily designed. The full organ, for example, would be used for slow, sustained and dignified music, as befitted the end of the service.

The English organ

Little is known about the development of the pipe organ in England from the building of the instrument in Winchester Cathedral in AD *c*.990 until the early sixteenth century. Given the Benedictine order's interest in music and organs, there must have been organs in at least some of their other churches and cathedrals in England before the Reformation. There are occasional references in surviving medieval documents to the installation or the restoration of instruments (York Minster in 1147, Westminster Abbey in 1304). In many cases more than one instrument is mentioned, suggesting that organs were placed in various parts of the church to accompany different services or different parts of the same service. It is also known that organ builders from continental Europe worked in England in the fifteenth and sixteenth centuries. In 1457, for example, a Dutch friar named John Roose is said to have built an organ for York Minster. By the fifteenth century there

was a Guild of 'Orgelmakers', though this was dissolved in 1531.

The earliest significant documentation concerning organ building in England dates from 1519. In that year Antony Duddington built an organ for All Hallows Church, Barking, Essex, with a standard manual compass for the time of 27 natural keys (white notes) and a full principal chorus. Whether or not the principal ranks could be separated by stops is not known. There may have been stopped bass pipes, possibly played by pedals, as in continental organs of the period.

The Thomas Thamar organ now in St Michael's Church, Framlingham, Suffolk. The organ was originally built for Pembroke College, Cambridge, and transferred to Framlingham when a new instrument was built in the eighteenth century. The case is reputedly pre-Restoration.

The Organ

The two-manual organ at Oriel College, Oxford, with 20 stops and mechanical action, was built in 1988 by J. W. Walker and Sons.

A few sixteenth- and early seventeenth-century English organ cases survive (Framlingham, Suffolk; King's College, Cambridge; Old Radnor, Powys; Tewkesbury Abbey, Gloucestershire) but little is known about their original contents. The construction and ornamentation of the cases suggest both French and Dutch/Flemish influences. Records of instruments built in England later in the sixteenth century suggest that the specifications were closer to Italian styles than French or Germanic ones. As far as can be determined, few if any English organs built in either the fifteenth or the sixteenth century had pedals. Mixtures were rarely included until the 1660s and all the ranks, however small, could be controlled separately, as in Italy. Reed stops were also rare until the seventeenth century, even though the regal was a popular instrument at the Tudor and Elizabethan courts.

English organs did often have two manuals, however. There are many references to the construction of 'double organs' and, indeed, compositions such as the *Voluntaries for Double Organ* by John Lugge, organist of Exeter Cathedral early in the seventeenth century, require a two-manual organ but do not need pedals. Many of these two-manual instruments had Great and Chair divisions, though sometimes the second division was placed inside the main case with the Great organ. A large English organ built in the 1650s, though probably by a continental builder, survives at Adlington Hall, Cheshire. There are two manuals, a large Great division with each rank separable from the others, and a small Choir division of only three stops placed inside the main case and sharing its Stopped Diapason pipes with those of the Great division. There are three reed stops and there is a suggestion that at some point an attempt was made to fit pedal pull-downs.

During the Commonwealth period (1649-60) most church organs were either destroyed or removed from their original location. The organ at Magdalen College, Oxford, built some time after 1615, was presented to Oliver Cromwell, who had the instrument removed in 1654 to Hampton Court, where the poet Milton is said to have played it. The organ was returned to Oxford in 1661. It was moved to Tewkesbury Abbey in 1737. Some in-

The organ of St James, Clerkenwell, London, a two-manual organ. Case by George Pike England, 1792; restored by Noel Mander, 1978.

Left: *The organ at the Royal Scottish Academy of Music and Drama, Glasgow, built in 1988 by J. W. Walker and Sons. It has two manuals, 22 stops and mechanical action.*

Right: *The organ at the church of St James without the Priory Gates at Southwick, Hampshire, has one manual, five stops and mechanical action. It was built by J. W. Walker and Sons in 1984.*

struments were stored away for protection until the Restoration of the Monarchy; others were moved into taverns to accompany the singing there!

Between the end of the English Civil War and the Restoration of the Monarchy, a number of English organ builders worked in northern France. Here they were influenced by the French style of organ building and brought new ideas back to England with them in the 1660s, when organs were once more allowed in churches and organ builders were in demand. Foremost amongst the French-influenced builders was Renatus Harris, one of a long line of English organ builders. Few of his organs survive in their

original form, even though by the time of his death in 1721 he had built at least six organs for cathedrals and many more for parish churches. His largest organ was at Salisbury Cathedral, where the instrument had four manuals, though the fourth keyboard controlled only a selection of stops from the Great division. The organ may have had pedal pull-downs.

Bernhard Smith was Harris's archrival. The two organ builders even contested a 'battle of organs' at the Temple Church in London, to see which of them should receive the contract to build an organ for that prestigious church. Smith won, perhaps because he introduced

Above: *The organ at Bolton Town Hall, Lancashire. Built by J. W. Walker and Sons in 1985, it has four manuals, 43 stops and mechanical action. The organ replaced an earlier instrument destroyed by fire.*

many ranks new to England from Germany and Holland, where it is thought that he trained as an organ builder. His most famous instrument was at St Paul's Cathedral, built between 1695 and 1697.

Smith and Harris introduced mixtures, cornets, mutations and reed stops into English organs as standard parts of the specification. Apart from a few instances where pedal pull-downs were included, there was no pedal division and no pedal keyboard. The manual keyboards were longer than on the continent, with four or more additional notes at the bass end of the manuals, more than was customary on the continent. This would help the organist to provide depth to the sound. The Great and Chair or Choir divisions were the

norm until the end of the eighteenth century. Third manuals were normally called Echo in late seventeenth- and early eighteenth-century English organs. The Echo division was normally of short compass, like the French organ's Récit manual. On occasion this division was enclosed in a box to make the sound more distant. Swell shutters were introduced early in the eighteenth century, probably by Abraham Jordan in his instrument for St Magnus the Martyr, London Bridge. Jordan imported sherry from Spain, where he discovered the idea for swell shutters of some kind. Early swell mechanisms were operated by a rope fitted to a pedal near the player's feet. The lever which operated the shutters in front of the box itself looked

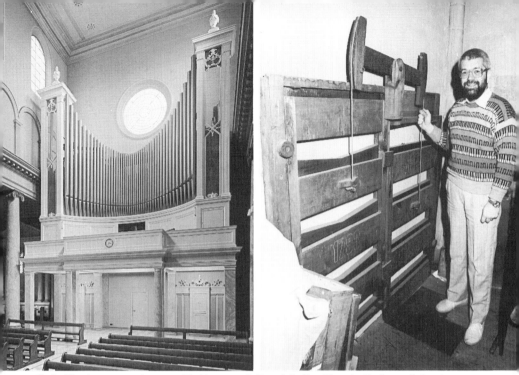

Left: *The three-manual organ with 46 stops at St Peter's Italian Church, Clerkenwell, London, was originally built in 1886 by Anneessen of Grammont, Belgium, but was rebuilt in 1957 by J. W. Walker and Sons. It has electric action.*

Right: *The author with the 'nag's head swell' mechanism of the Wymondham Abbey organ.*

like a child's hobby-horse, hence the nickname 'nag's head swell' which is often given to early swell mechanisms.

Apart from the introduction of the Swell division and mechanism, English organ building followed much the same style as that created by Harris and Smith, remaining relatively small (maximum three manuals and 25 stops), with no pedals and few, if any, manual couplers. The Chair division, as on the continent, gradually disappeared, being replaced by a division in the main case of the instrument. These changes apart, an organ built at the end of the eighteenth century in England would have been easily recognisable to a late seventeenth-century organ builder.

A small number of organ builders dominated English organ building in the eighteenth century. Only the larger churches and cathedrals possessed organs, though these were often a matter of much local pride and occasionally dispute. When John Snetzler, a Swiss organ builder who spent most of his working life in England, built a large organ for Halifax Parish Church, West Yorkshire, in 1764-6, many of the local townspeople boycotted its use, claiming that it was too expensive. It took two years of wrangling in the ecclesiastical courts before the instrument could be used!

The organ at Halifax was typical of those instruments built in English churches and cathedrals during the late

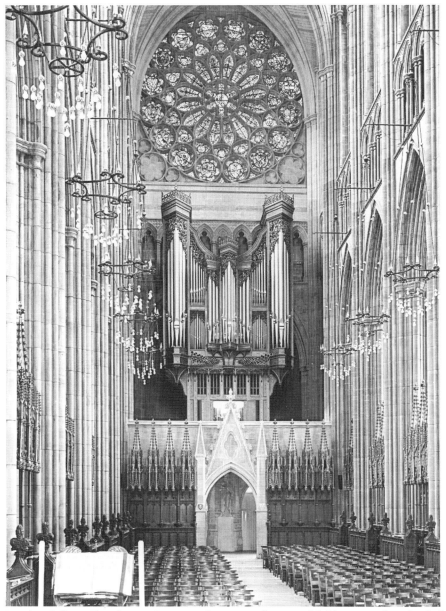

Lancing College Chapel, West Sussex: a four-manual organ with 54 stops and mechanical action built by J. W. Walker and Sons in 1986. Note the horizontal reed pipes.

The Organ

The organ of Trinity College, Dublin, Ireland, built by J. W. Walker and Sons in 1967 (originally by Samuel Green c.1790). It is a three-manual organ with 25 stops and mechanical action.

History and types

seventeenth and eighteenth centuries. It replaced a small band who had previously led the singing of the services. In smaller country churches, many of these bands continued into the nineteenth century, though virtually all had been wound up by 1850. Thomas Hardy's novel *Under the Greenwood Tree* tells the story of how a village church band was replaced by a pipe organ.

The Halifax Parish Church organ was placed on a gallery at the west end of the church. Its specification is shown in the table overleaf.

There were no couplers or pedals. The compass of the Great and Choir manuals

The parish church, St Michael's, Ashton-under-Lyne, Lancashire: the organ by William Hill, 1845, rebuilt in 1962 by J. W. Walker and Sons, has three manuals, 48 stops and electric action. As originally built, the organ was modelled on German instruments, complete with pedal organ.

began three natural keys lower than present-day keyboards. The Swell division began sixteen natural keys above the bottom note on a modern manual keyboard. The swell shutters would be controlled by the nag's head movement referred to earlier. The Cornet stop was mounted above the rest of the Great pipework on its own separate windchest. The Sesquialtera was a particular kind of mixture with a Tierce rank in its composition, the term denoting the relationship between that rank and the others in the stop. Hautboy is another name for Oboe. The organ was extensively rebuilt in the nineteenth and twentieth centuries and now contains only a few pipes from the original organ. The first organist was William Herschel, who later became Astronomer Royal.

The organ in America

Organs were erected in America as early as the sixteenth century. These

The five-manual organ by Noel Mander in Birmingham Town Hall, based on the William Hill organ of 1834, with additions in 1843, 1890 and 1933. The instrument was the first to contain a high-pressure solo reed.

GREAT ORGAN		CHOIR ORGAN	
Open Diapason	8	Open Diapason	8
Open Diapason	8	Stopped Diapason	8
Stopped Diapason	8	Principal	4
Principal	4	Flute	4
Twelfth	3	Fifteenth	2
Fifteenth	2	Bassoon	8
Sesquialtera	IV	Vox Humana	8
Furniture	III		
Cornet	V	SWELL ORGAN	
Trumpet	8	Open Diapason	8
Clarion	4	Stopped Diapason	8
		Principal	4
		Sesquialtera	III
		Hautboy	8
		Trumpet	8

Specification of the Halifax Parish Church organ.

instruments were imported from Spain and Portugal for the cathedrals and monasteries of the Iberian colonies. Organs imported from France existed in Quebec churches as early as 1660. A number of organs were brought from Germany to Pennsylvania in the eighteenth century by the colonists there, and a similar import of organs from England took place in New England at the same time. All these instruments were small.

By *c.*1750 organs were being built in North America, in eastern Pennsylvania and Boston. Pennsylvanian organs followed German models, while those built in Boston were copies of English eighteenth-century instruments. It was not until well into the nineteenth century that organ builders in America adopted the more modern styles and techniques of construction and tonal design then prevalent in Europe.

The organ after 1800

By the beginning of the nineteenth century organ-building styles were starting to change. Composers such as Beethoven, Berlioz and Liszt sought vivid means of expression. The Werkprinzip organ in particular gave way to instruments which aimed to provide the organist with an orchestra at his fingertips. Organ builders placed greater emphasis on extremes of sound and an ability to build up tone colours from combinations of 8 and 4 foot stops. Solo registers became more important than chorus ranks in many instruments. Because of its capacity for dynamic change, the swell box increased in importance during the course of the nineteenth century. More and more of the stops and the divisions were enclosed. In some cases the whole instrument was placed in a swell box.

These changes in the tonal design and layout of the organ were common throughout Europe. The Werkprinzip tradition was maintained to a certain extent in the Germanic countries where it had always been most influential, with fewer stops being enclosed than in instruments elsewhere. Organs became larger and louder, nevertheless.

In France organ building in the nineteenth century was dominated by Aristide Cavaillé-Coll, who built or re-

The Organ

The single-manual organ built by J. W. Walker and Sons in 1982 for the Catholic Church of Our Lady of Good Counsel at Horsforth, Leeds. It has eight stops.

built most of the major instruments in that country between 1841 and the end of the century. He continued the emphasis placed on reed stops by earlier French builders and introduced new varieties of stop such as the Gamba and the Celeste. However, he retained the chorus and some of the mutation stops of the eighteenth-century French organ. A great many of Cavaillé-Coll's instruments remain much as he left them. The largest relatively unaltered organ is at the basilica of St Sulpice, Paris. Charles-Marie Widor played here for many years. The Cavaillé-Coll organ at St Clotilde, Paris, inspired its organist, César Franck, to produce some of the finest music for the instrument composed in the nineteenth century.

For a short period from about 1840 to 1860 English organs led the field in tonal design. Through the work of H. J. Gauntlett, who studied organ building on the continent, and William Hill, one of the major English organ builders of the nineteenth century, a new kind of instrument emerged, capable of playing both the classical repertoire epitomised by the music of J. S. Bach and the new romantic compositions. The Hill/Gauntlett organ had complete choruses on the Great, Swell, Pedal and (to a lesser extent) Choir divisions, and a wide range of solo stops and mutations. Unlike many other English builders of the period, Hill respected older organs, rebuilding them sympathetically. Unfortunately many of his pioneering instruments have themselves been rebuilt. The Ulster Hall, Belfast, contains a large four-manual concert organ by Hill.

Hill built the first large town-hall organ at Birmingham in 1834. The town-hall organ came to the fore at a time when there were few orchestras and the only way in which people could hear symphonic music was through transcriptions for organ. The instrument became a one-man band capable of synthesising the various parts of the orchestra. In later town-hall organs the stops included percussion effects such as drums, cymbals and bird whistles. There was nothing new in this: large seventeenth- and eighteenth-century organs in Germany, for instance, contained similar effects such as the Cymbelstern, as noted earlier.

Most English town halls built in the nineteenth century had an organ installed in their concert auditorium. Many of these grand instruments still survive. The largest, at the Royal Albert Hall in London, has over 120 stops. Many of the stops, especially the reed ranks, are on high wind pressures. Originally built by Henry Willis, one of the great organ builders of the nineteenth century, the Albert Hall organ was rebuilt in the 1920s by the firm of Harrison and Harrison, one of the most renowned builders of the twentieth century. Concert-hall organs such as this have had to provide music for a wide range of functions, including interludes between boxing matches!

Hill, Willis and Harrison built or rebuilt most of the major concert, town-hall and cathedral organs in Britain. While their instruments retained the basic choruses of the eighteenth-century organ, they further developed solo stops and choruses of reeds. They were influenced in different ways by some of the

The Organ

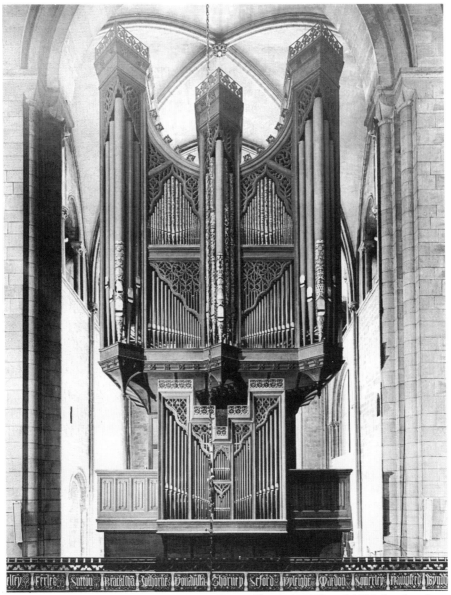

Chichester Cathedral organ, largely by William Hill, 1851, 1859 and 1888, but based on earlier work by Harris and Byfield and restored by Noel Mander in 1985. It includes a 'nave' section. The smaller organ case is for the functional Chair organ.

continental builders of the day, notably Cavaillé-Coll and the famous nineteenth-century German firm of Schulze. Schulze exported a number of instruments to Britain. The firm's flute stops, usually made of wood, and powerful principal choruses made a considerable impact on British organ building for several generations. The Schulze organs at Doncaster Parish Church and St Bartholomew's Church, Armley, Leeds, remain much as the builder left them. Schulze himself is reputed to have been influenced by the work of the Silbermann family.

In order to assist the player to control larger instruments, organ builders invented tubular-pneumatic and electro-pneumatic actions which lightened the key touch and enabled stops to be changed quickly. The very first pneumatic action, known as Barker lever after its inventor, C. S. Barker, combined tracker action with pneumatic motors which lightened the touch of the keys, especially when manuals were coupled together. A number of registration aids were also developed, many of them in England. In their crudest form such aids were simple shifting movements which shut off wind to certain stops, thus saving the organist the trouble of pushing or pulling the stopknobs in or out. In the early nineteenth century an English organ builder, J. C. Bishop, invented composition pedals. These were foot pedals, usually made of metal, which activated a series of levers which pushed out a particular group of stops. With electric and pneumatic actions, these pedals were replaced by pistons which activated the stops either electrically or pneumatically. In his organ for the Great Exhibition of 1851 Henry Willis placed small pistons between the manual keys so that the organist could change stops while playing simply by pressing the pistons with his thumbs. Most modern organs have such registration aids. Where the mechanism is electrically controlled, the pistons can be changed at will by the organist by means of setter switches attached to the piston system. Foot pistons on French organs are called *champignons* because they look like mushrooms!

For much of the twentieth century the English cathedral organ, as built by Harrison and Harrison, was regarded as the ideal instrument, emulated the world over. Many cathedral and large church organs still follow the basic Harrison design, first used at Ely Cathedral in 1908. Probably the best known of the Harrison instruments is at King's College, Cambridge. The organ case at King's College is one of the few pre-Restoration cases still existing. The instrument is typical of many organs in Britain especially, having been rebuilt and enlarged several times.

North American organ builders emulated British and German makers from the 1870s onwards. The large organ of the Boston Music Hall, built by Walcker of Ludwigsburg, Germany, greatly influenced American organ builders, setting a trend for bigger organs. A number of very large instruments were built in North America in the nineteenth and twentieth centuries, including the largest organ in the world at Atlantic City, New Jersey, with seven manuals and over thirty thousand pipes.

The Organ

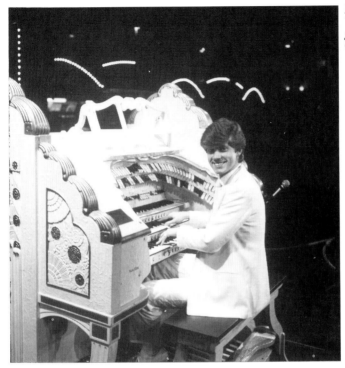

Other types of organ

If the concert-hall organ was a development of the nineteenth century, then the cinema or theatre organ was a product of the twentieth century. Until films had soundtracks, there was a need for some form of accompaniment to complement the silent motion pictures which were shown in cinemas. The organ, as a one-man band, was the ideal instrument to provide such accompaniment. With electric action, the pipes could be fitted in anywhere around the auditorium. It had a wide range of sounds and tone colours and an endless range of special effects, from bird whistles to thunder pedals and from foghorns to church bells, all of which could be used to enhance the drama of the film.

Initially, theatre and cinema organs were much the same as church or concert-hall instruments. A different and distinct style of design and construction soon emerged, however. The pioneer of the cinema organ was Robert Hope-Jones (1859-1914). He patented new forms of electric action and changed the organ's tonal design from one in which a series of choruses forms the basis of the sound to one where loud 16, 8 and 4 foot stops are the only ranks required. Hope-Jones's first instruments were for churches, including a large four-manual instrument built for Worcester Cathedral in 1896. His mechanical inventions required a better supply of electricity than was generally available at the end of the nineteenth century and many of his instruments soon became unplayable. He survived bankruptcy, however, and emigrated to the United States, where his business interests were acquired by the Wurlitzer organ company, which developed Hope-Jones's ideas into the cinema organ.

In most cinema organs all the stops were enclosed in swell boxes as a means of maximising the expressive capabilities of the instrument. New ranks were developed. These included the Tibia, a large-scale, heavily blown flute stop, and the Kinura, a keen-sounding reed rank. In order to increase the range of the instrument, each rank of pipes was extended over a number of pitches. Thus a register might appear at 16, 8, 4, $2^2/3$, 2 and $1^3/5$ foot pitches, and on more than one manual. The principle of extension of ranks was also used in many church and concert organs in the first half of the twentieth century, especially by the John Compton Organ Company. The characteristic sound of the cinema organ comes from the use of the Tremulant. While in most church and concert-hall organs the Tremulant is used only occasionally, usually in combination with a solo stop or stops, the Tremulants on a cinema organ are in almost constant use. They are intended to provide the equivalent of the vibrato on a stringed instrument.

Once 'talking' films arrived, the cinema organ lost its popularity and in the 1950s and 1960s many instruments were removed from their original homes and often scrapped altogether. Some have been rebuilt in new surroundings, where they are still regularly used. The organ museum at Thursford, Norfolk, houses one of the largest cinema organs still playable in Britain. One of the few cinema organs remaining in its original home is that built by Wurlitzer for the Tower Ballroom, Blackpool. Like many cinema organs, the instrument has a 'resident' organist. Reginald Dixon was for many years organist there, though unlike many of his fellow organists he accompanied dancing rather than films.

Pipe organs were also found in private houses. The organ had long been a secular instrument, and there are references to organs at the courts of medieval and Renaissance monarchs and in the homes of princes and rich merchants. Such organs were always small. There would normally be only a limited amount of space to house the instrument and the music played on these house organs would not be complex — they were for the owners rather than professional musicians to play. The organ at Adlington Hall, Cheshire, was larger than most. Much more typical is the small instrument in Carisbrooke Castle, Isle of Wight. Built at the end of the sixteenth century by a continental organ builder, it is the oldest playable organ in Britain. It has no pedals, one manual of a relatively short compass of 45 notes and three stops: flute ranks of 4 foot and 2 foot pitch and an 8 foot Regal.

Many house or chamber organs were built in the eighteenth century and a good many instruments survive in country houses. Many were built in Britain

The Organ

Left: *The chamber organ at Carisbrooke Castle, Isle of Wight, by Hoffheimer, 1602. Reputedly played by Princess Elizabeth, daughter of King Charles I, this organ can still be played today.*

Right: *An example of a cabinet organ, built by Mander, 1981.*

by the main church-organ builders such as Smith, Harris and Snetzler. These instruments usually had only one manual and no pedals, a principal chorus up to 2 foot pitch, a Cornet stop and possibly a solo reed rank. A number of the stops would draw in two parts so that, even though the organ had only one keyboard, a solo could be played with the right hand by drawing only the upper part of the stop.

Chamber organs would be used for private practice and entertainment. Small organs were also used in churches on the continent to accompany small services or as part of the orchestra, fulfilling the continuo role, filling out the instrumental parts. Just as people demonstrated their wealth by building large church or concert-hall organs, so many rich people installed organs in their own homes. The Schulze organ now at Armley, for instance, though a large four-manual instrument with a bold principal chorus, was originally a house organ.

Some organs have no pipes at all. In the late twentieth century the electronic organ has developed, in which sounds are produced like those of an instrument with pipes but by electronic means. The advantage of the electronic organ is that it saves space and, though it has a shorter life than a well made pipe organ, it needs less maintenance. Electronic organs are popular as house instruments, though even here there is now a renaissance in pipe-organ construction. The most up-to-date electronic organs, controlled by microchips, can produce a wide range of sounds at the touch of a button and sound very much like real pipe organs.

The 'American organ' or harmonium has no pipes, except perhaps dummy ones. Its characteristic reedy sound is made from small reeds inside the instrument. In a sense, it is the descendant of the regal, described earlier. The harmonium became very popular as a house instrument and in small churches and chapels. It still survives in some country churches as the only accompaniment to services.

Some organs have pipes but no keyboards. Mechanical organs, most familiar as barrel organs, have been made for several centuries. Queen Elizabeth I sent the royal organ builder, Dallam, to Turkey to build a mechanical organ for the Sultan. The principle is the same as with a standard pipe organ. The difference is that, instead of keyboards and fingers,

The Schulze organ in St Bartholomew's Church, Armley, Leeds; four-manual, 1869.

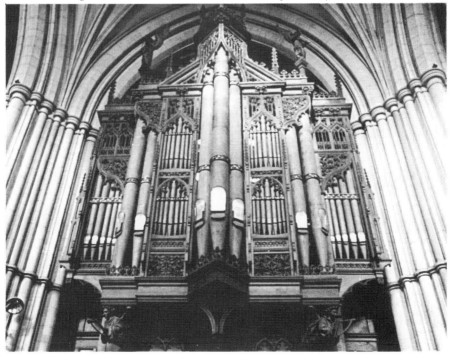

The Organ

The modern organ at the Church of St John, Chelsea, London, built by Mander in 1978.

with perforations which correspond to the notes of music. Some of the holes activate stop changes. There were many barrel organs in churches in the nineteenth century simply because there was no organist. Some music was written especially for mechanical organs. Haydn wrote pieces, for example, while Mozart composed two large-scale fantasias for the instrument, though they are such grand compositions that they must have strained the mechanism and are played nowadays by an organist.

Modern organ design

In recent years organ builders have returned to the styles of the seventeenth and eighteenth centuries, copying the Werkprinzip organs described earlier in this chapter. Many instruments are now built with tracker action and a stoplist similar to that used by J. S. Bach and his contemporaries. The organ at the Royal Festival Hall, London, was the first major British organ of the twentieth century to use eighteenth-century stoplists and pipe voicing, though the action was electro-pneumatic rather than tracker. The organ at Queen's College, Oxford, built by the Danish organ builder Frobenius was the first truly Werkprinzip organ built in Britain. Such organs have been built again in Germany since the 1920s, when Albert Schweitzer, amongst others, drew attention to the many old organs still surviving. Schweitzer persuaded organ builders to return to eighteenth-century styles of organ design and construction. The resulting neo-classical type of organ has been adopted as the model for church and concert-hall organs in

the instrument is played by a mechanical device which pulls the pallets under the windchest at the right time. The construction of barrel or mechanical organs is similar to that of a mechanical clock. Typically, a barrel with spikes or holes in it matches up with the mechanism of the instrument. Each spike or hole corresponds to a note on the instrument and whenever it comes round on the barrel the note plays. In fairground organs the pallets are activated by folding cards

History and types

Europe and North America. In France there has also been a return to the styles of the eighteenth century, though the work of Cavaillé-Coll has also been preserved. The remaining historic organs in Britain are gradually being carefully restored to their original condition wherever possible. Much work remains to be done to restore the classical organs of Spain, Portugal and Italy.

Pipe organs are still regularly built or rebuilt throughout the world. Large organs of over one hundred stops have been built in countries as far apart as the United States, Australia and Hong Kong. At the other end of the scale, small one- or two-manual instruments, with only a few stops, are also still built in many churches, schools, concert rooms and homes.

Left: A modern organ built in 1989 by Peter Collins, Leicester, after the style of the Strasbourg Silbermanns, for the International Organ Festival, St Albans.

Right: The modern house organ at Chalfont Heights, Buckinghamshire, built in 1973 by Peter Collins.

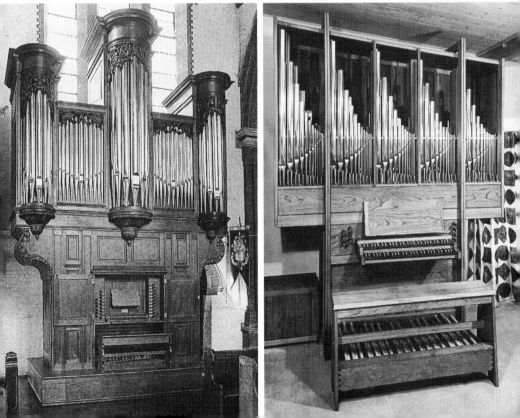

The Organ

Under construction in 1989 at the factory of J. W. Walker and Sons at Brandon, Suffolk, is an organ for the church of St Martin-in-the-Fields, London. The organ follows the Werkprinzip arrangement of divisions and stops.

3
Technique and repertoire

Technique

Unlike any other musical instrument, the organ can sustain sound indefinitely. A note played on a piano will die away as the string inside the instrument gradually stops vibrating after being struck by the hammer attached to the key. A note played on a woodwind or brass instrument will sound only as long as the player has breath in his or her lungs. But an organ pipe will sound without any loss of power or change in timbre until the player chooses to stop depressing the manual or pedal key.

Because of this sustaining quality the playing technique required for the organ is markedly different from that for both the harpsichord and the piano. In order to make a smooth transition from one note to another, the organist must ensure that there is neither too great nor too small a gap between the point where wind stops entering one pipe and the point where wind enters the next. In many cases the player must change fingers or feet while depressing the same key or pedal in order to ensure a smooth sound.

An organist has only two feet (as opposed to ten fingers) so that, while many notes can be played on the manuals at the same time, only two or, at most, three notes can be depressed by either the toe or the heel of the foot at any one point. The same principle of smooth playing applies to the pedal part as to the manual parts of a piece of music. The organist has to learn to play the correct pedal notes without looking down at the feet. This takes time and a good deal of practice, though eventually it becomes second nature in the way that changing gear on a car is an automatic procedure, carried out without thinking by the experienced driver.

The player has to be able to co-ordinate the hands and feet so that, for example, three different melodies can be played at the same time — one in the right hand, the second in the left hand and the third in the pedals. Trio sonatas such as those by J. S. Bach require this complete independence of the hands and feet.

An important aspect of playing the organ is the selection and manipulation of the stops — the art of registration, as it is called. Organs vary considerably in size and tonal design, and the location of the instrument can have an important effect on the sound. In large churches, for instance, there may be an echo of several seconds after a pipe has ceased to sound. This has to be taken into account when playing if the music is not to sound so blurred that it becomes unrecognisable.

Because a pipe sounds the moment air is let into its foot and stops sounding as soon as the pallet closes, the organist has to take great care when adding or subtracting stops. In general, the registration is not altered while the stops on which the music is being played are sounding, but stops can be changed on one or more divisions while music is being played on another.

On a piano the player increases or decreases the volume by depressing the keys (and hence the strings) with more or less force as appropriate. The only ways in which the volume can be increased or decreased on the organ are either to add or reduce the number of stops in use or to use the swell box, where available. In practice, both techniques are often used together.

The way in which the sound is built up or reduced will depend on the particular instrument, the specification and the way in which the stops are voiced. In organ music written before about 1850 gradations in power normally take the form of a series of steps up or down in volume, given the Werkprinzip design of most instruments and the lack of swell boxes of any size. Indeed, much music would be played throughout on the same stop combinations. Because of the lack of registration aids and the cumbersome size of the stopknobs, an assistant would be required for rapid changes of registration.

Music written after 1850 places much more emphasis on finely graded crescendos and diminuendos, which can be properly achieved only with larger swell boxes and combination pedals or pistons. With a Swell division or divisions, even unenclosed ranks can be made to increase or decrease in volume if they are coupled to ranks which are enclosed. The organist's skill in gradually building up or reducing the volume is in knowing which ranks to add or subtract and at what point to open or close the swell box or boxes.

The registration of a piece of music will be determined not only by the instrument on which it is to be played but also by the historic conventions associated with the composition, as well as the player's personal taste and approach. We can only guess how early organs sounded and therefore do not know for certain which stops to use for the music which would have been played on them. However, where instruments survive which are contemporary with a particular composer or a school of composition, it is important to discover how they were used in order to give as authentic a performance as possible on other instruments.

Chapter 2 described the various styles of organ building. Until the eighteenth century it was virtually unknown for a piece of organ music to contain any instructions regarding the registration to be used. We do know with some degree of certainty how music from *c*.1680 onwards was to be registered. To a certain extent the instrument's limitations dictated the way in which the stops were used. Instruments were hand-blown and the channels through which the wind was led from the bellows to the windchest were often narrow. It would not normally be possible, therefore, to use all the stops together — there simply would not be enough wind for them all!

In any case, it is not necessary for all the registers to sound together in order to increase the volume. If a loud stop is added to a softer stop, then the sound of the softer stop is masked. Even if two stops of the same volume are added together, the sound output does not double in volume.

Technique and repertoire

Increasing the power of the registration normally comes from adding stops of different pitches. Only one stop of each pitch is required in any combination of stops unless flue and reed stops are to be used together or there is a specific reason to make an exception to this convention. In many organs the largest pipes of the main principal rank on the Great and possibly Pedal divisions are often displayed in the front of the case. The air has to be brought specially to these ranks from tubes conveyanced off the main windchest. This tends to make the pipes speak less quickly than those on the windchest itself. In order to improve responsiveness, a second 8 foot stop on the main windchest is added to the rank whose pipes are in the case. This usually covers up any irregularities in the sound. We also saw in Chapter 1 how two 8 foot stops are deliberately made out of tune with each other in order to give a 'beating' effect.

Unless a special and unusual effect is being sought, the basis of any combination will be an 8 foot stop on the manual and a 16 foot stop on the pedal. 16 foot stops are often found on manual divisions and, when used, can add depth and grandeur to the sound. Conversely, using pedal stops of 8 foot pitch and above without a 16 foot or a 32 foot stop being added lightens the sound and provides a contrast to the normal pedal combinations. 4 foot stops are occasionally used on their own (some very small instruments do not have an 8 foot stop on all the manuals) or in combination with other higher-pitched stops. Above 4 foot pitch, stops are used only in combination with lower-pitched ranks, either as

part of a chorus of principals or flutes, or to 'colour' the lower ranks to form a sound combination which will enable a solo melody to be played. Mutation stops (described in earlier chapters) are used in this way. Single stops, normally of 8 foot pitch, can also be used on their own for softer sounds. Stops on the same division can be combined with each other or with stops on other manuals and the pedals, using couplers, where available.

Where the music is chordal (where several notes are played at the same time), the stops used tend to be either the full flue chorus, with or without the reed stops, or possibly the reed stops on their own, or (in some circumstances) the 8 foot principal or Diapason stops alone. Such stop combinations can also be used for contrapuntal music, where one or more tunes are combined in different ways. However, in order to ensure that the tune or tunes can be clearly heard at all times, the organist has to ensure that the combination of stops used produces a clear sound. This is normally best done by using stops of the same kind (as for example the principal stops) at different pitches.

In trio sonatas (already referred to) and similar music where two or more different melodies are combined, it is important to ensure that each melody 'stands out' as it is being played. The organist will therefore use contrasting stops, on different manuals and the pedals, for each melodic line. One hand, for example, might be playing on a manual controlling a reed stop, the other on a manual controlling two flute stops of different pitches, while the pedals were controlling a single 8 foot principal stop. These stops are different in timbre but approximately equal in volume.

In much organ music, however, one melody is meant to be heard more prominently than the others. Organs have a range of solo stops and solo combinations for this purpose. Indeed, as we saw in chapter 1, large instruments have a whole division of such ranks. The accompaniment will be played on another manual and the pedals, using softer flute or principal stops expressly voiced for the purpose.

One of the earliest known registration instructions is *organo pleno* or 'full organ'. The nature and sound of 'full organ' varies according to country and style of organ building. On one instrument it is possible to have more than one 'full organ' sound. The 'full organ' of the classical Werkprinzip instrument as played by J. S. Bach would normally consist of the full principal chorus on the main manual (Hauptwerk), with the full principal chorus on the pedals, plus the pedal reeds. In large instruments the two main manuals might be coupled together for the *organo pleno*. To provide a contrast to this sound, parts of the piece might be played on a subsidiary chorus of stops on another division. The 'full organ' sound might be coloured with reed stops on the manual divisions, especially if the music was chordal rather than contrapuntal, and with any principal-scaled mutation ranks or Cornet stops.

In chapter 2 reference was made to the registration conventions of the French organ before about 1840. Here, full organ would be described as the 'Plein Jeu'. This would usually consist of the principal chorus on the Great division (Grande Orgue), possibly coupled to the principal chorus on the Positif, known as the 'Petit Plein Jeu'. Alternatively, the 'full organ' might consist of the 'Grand Jeu'. Here, the loud reeds on the Grande Orgue (or possibly the Bombarde division, if one existed) would be drawn along with the 4 foot Principal stop and the Cornet. The Cornet would help to maintain the power of the reed stops in the upper part of their compass. A French organist would know which stops to use when he saw one or other of these terms written in the music. Indeed, some of the titles of the pieces refer to the registration, as for example 'Offertoire sur les Grands Jeux'.

Because French organs of the late seventeenth and eighteenth centuries were all built according to the same design, it was possible to develop standard registration instructions for music played on them. At the head of much French organ music of this period is a phrase (for example 'Grand Jeu') which would mean the same to any French organist, whichever organ he was playing. Registration instructions, apart from those for full organ, included directions on which stops to draw for a Trumpet or Cornet solo or a combination of mutation stops which included a Twelfth, Seventeenth and possibly a Nineteenth rank, or other reed- and flue-stop solos or combinations.

Similar registration instructions or conventions can be found in English organ music of the same period. The term 'Full Organ', for example, would result in the player drawing the Open and Stopped Diapasons, the Principal,

Technique and repertoire

Twelfth, Fifteenth and all Mixture stops on the Great Organ. If specially instructed, and there was enough wind, the Trumpet and Clarion stops would also be added. None of the manuals would be coupled together. The term 'Diapasons' would instruct the player to use the Open and Stopped Diapasons together. Other directions would tell the organist which solo stop to use (for example, Trumpet, Flute, Vox Humana) or occasionally which manual to play on (for example Swell or Echo).

In general, however, references to particular stops or stop combinations before about 1850 are rare. Very few of J. S. Bach's organ compositions contain any registration instructions and these may well not be original. It is clear from the texture of the music that some pieces require balanced combinations on each division while others need a solo stop or stops with accompaniment. Pedal solos would normally use stops of 8 foot or 4 foot pitch. Reed stops were often available at these pitches; their penetrating sound enables them to be more easily heard against the manual stops than a flute or a principal rank would be.

When performing older organ compositions, organists must also be aware of conventions relating to the playing of the notes themselves. Because music had to be written out by hand, a kind of musical shorthand developed which saved time. Organists would know what was intended by composer, even though not all the notes or rhythms were written out in full. The conventions used in this musical shorthand varied from country to country and period to period. One of the best known types of shorthand is the French system of *notes inégales* (unequal notes). Here, though the notation might seem to suggest that all the notes are played evenly, the convention of the time dictates that the notes should be played unevenly — not of equal length — the first note of a pair being longer than the second.

After about 1850 composers of organ music became much more precise in their registration instructions. Many were players themselves and they often required a particular effect when their music was being performed. As in earlier periods, French organ registration was very stylised, especially since most of the major instruments were built or rebuilt by one person, Aristide Cavaillé-Coll. A direction to use the reeds or the full chorus on any instrument built by

François Couperin: 'Messe...des Paroisses'. Eighteenth-century French organ music was written and played according to certain specific conventions. One of these was the use of 'notes inégales'. Though written out as equal notes (left), the player would know to play the quavers of the piece as dotted quaver followed by semiquaver — as unequal notes (right).

him would result in almost exactly the same sound being produced. His instruments were built on the understanding that different timbres would be produced by combining stops of the same pitch. The instruction 'Fonds' (foundation stops), for example, would direct the organist to use three or more 8 foot stops together. A gradual crescendo could be achieved by coupling the manuals together and either adding stops or having the stops already drawn letting wind into them only when required. This was possible through use of a ventil mechanism. The ventil was a block between the bellows and the part of the windchest which it controlled. With the ventil closed, wind could not reach the windchest and pipes would not sound, even if the stops had been drawn at the console and the sliders were correctly positioned over the windchest. With the ventil open, the wind could pass into the windchest and into any pipes whose sliders had been drawn.

In nineteenth-century German organs, crescendos and diminuendos were often achieved through a general crescendo pedal. As the pedal was depressed, the stops were added automatically, thus increasing the volume. Reversing the procedure reduced the sound. Much German organ music of the period relies on the organist's ability to move from the softest to the loudest combinations and back again.

Modern actions and registration aids (discussed in the two previous chapters) have enabled organists to change stops and sound levels or timbres rapidly. Certainly, when playing orchestral transcriptions or certain kinds of nineteenth- and twentieth-century organ music, the organist needs to be able to change registration rapidly. This is a relatively straightforward operation when foot and thumb pistons are available, particularly when the stop combinations which they activate can be adjusted to suit the requirements of the piece being played.

Repertoire

Most organs of any size built before the nineteenth century were located in churches. The music written for these instruments was inevitably linked with the liturgy and the services of that church. The simple medieval organs would have accompanied the plainchant singing, reinforcing the vocal lines. As instruments grew larger, more varied in tone and more sophisticated in operation, the organ became a solo as well as an accompanying instrument.

This section concentrates on the organ as a solo instrument. However, many organs today are still built to accompany singers, usually in church, and the pipes are constructed and voiced so that they can either accompany voices or other instruments or lead large congregations or choirs. The softer stops are useful for accompaniment, while the loud registers ensure that large numbers of singers are effectively supported. The principles of good accompanying are the same as those for effective solo playing: a sensitive approach to the music and the instrument; careful choice of registers, taking account of the organ, the building and the function; subtle change of stops when required; rhythmic playing and effective technique.

The church organ was used as a solo instrument in a number of ways. In the Roman Catholic mass it became customary for the organ to alternate with the singers or the priest in the performance of the plainsong. One section of the plainsong would be sung. The next would be played by the organist, who would embellish or vary the chant. The earliest variations would have been made up on the spot by the organist. The ability to improvise has remained an important part of the church organist's craft, for there are still many occasions during a service when music is required at short notice.

Much organ music is based on pre-existing melodies, whether plainsong, hymn melodies or other tunes, both secular and sacred. The *organ mass* consisted of a series of pieces which were to be played at various points in the communion service, normally in Catholic churches, and, as already noted, might alternate with singing. Some of the pieces in an organ mass would be based on plainsong — and especially those plainchant melodies which were sung during the course of the mass. The organ mass pieces embellished the plainsong tunes in the same way that German Protestant organists would embellish the chorale melodies as a prelude to the singing of the hymn. Organ mass and similar settings of plainsong, where the choir alternated with the organist, were also performed in England before the Protestant Reformation.

From the sixteenth century in the Protestant churches of Europe, if music was allowed in worship at all, the emphasis was on hymn singing rather than chanting. The chorales which were sung in Lutheran and other churches stimulated the composition of an extensive repertoire of solo organ music. Before a congregation sang a hymn or a chorale, some or all of the tune was played by the organist so that the people knew what to sing. This playing of the tune was thus a prelude to the congregation's singing of it. Chorale preludes varied considerably in style, ranging from the simple and meditative to the grand and brilliant. They were usually written so as to reflect the sentiments of the original words to which the melody was sung. Thus a chorale prelude based on a Christmas tune would be bright and joyful; one based on a Passiontide hymn would be sombre and reflective. The organist would be expected to choose appropriate stops when playing these pieces.

There were also many sets of 'chorale variations' for organ. Here, the basic melody was in effect rewritten in different ways. These variations may well have originated from the practice of improvising or embellishing existing melodies. Certainly they allowed the organist to demonstrate the various stops and combinations of the instrument as well as the player's virtuosity. The term **partita** (probably from the French *partie*, denoting a piece in several parts or sections) was sometimes used as the title of a set of variations for organ or other keyboard instrument.

A **passacaglia** (probably from the Spanish dance *pasacalle*) is also a set of variations, with a short musical phrase being repeated over and over again throughout the piece. The composer

The Organ

then varies the accompaniment to this melody. Many organ passacaglias have the repeated melody as the pedal part, with the embellishments in the manual parts. A **chaconne** is similar in structure, except that a chord progression rather than a melody is used as the basis of the variations.

Not all organ music is based on existing melodies such as chorale tunes or plainchant. Much of it is 'free' composition with themes written by the composer as the basis of the pieces.

The **toccata** is usually a piece with fast-moving scale passages. The pedal part, where it is included, may also move rapidly, often as a solo, showing off the organist's virtuosity. The word comes from the Italian *toccare*, 'to touch', the implication being that the keys have to be touched lightly or quickly.

A toccata may be played on its own or it may be linked with a **fugue**. A fugue is like a canon or a round, with the melody or theme being played on its own and then repeated against a countermelody until several musical parts are being played at the same time. A second melody may then appear in contrast to the first. This is also treated fugally. The first theme may then reappear in conjunction with the second one. In large organ fugues the themes are played by both hands and feet.

J. S. Bach: Toccata from 'Toccata and Fugue in D minor'. This work is probably the best known piece of organ music. The toccata is full of virtuoso writing for the hands and dramatic chords, as the opening few bars show. The speed, dynamic and registration markings are modern.

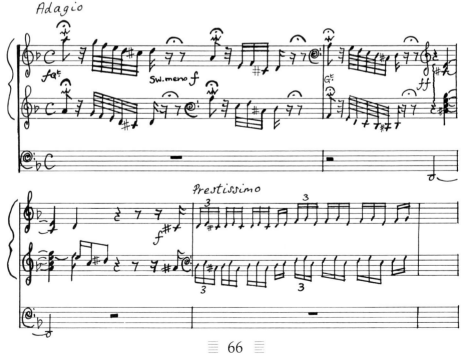

Technique and repertoire

J. S. Bach: Fugue from 'Toccata and Fugue in D minor'. Fugues usually begin with the statement of the fugue theme, after which it is repeated in two or more other parts, with a countermelody or melodies played against it, as shown above Finally, the fugue theme or subject appears in the pedals (below). The speed and dynamic markings are modern, as are the indications of which foot to use. A mark above the stave denotes use of the right foot, below the left. A 'u' denotes use of the heel, a '∧' the toe.

Fugues may be linked with other pieces, such as a **fantasia** or a **prelude**. A prelude simply precedes the fugue and may be in a variety of musical styles. A fantasia is usually free-ranging in character, often sounding like a well thought-out improvisation rather than a fully composed piece of music. It may, for example, combine majestic chords with virtuoso scales and arpeggios for the hands and feet.

There are many other forms of organ music. The term **sonata** has a long history and denotes many different kinds of piece. The word literally means 'sound-piece' and originally described a musical composition consisting of one movement only. By the eighteenth century, however, sonatas could have as many as three movements. Organ sonatas were modelled on the instrumental trio sonatas, with their fast-slow-fast sections. By the beginning of the nineteenth century the sonata normally had four movements.

The term **voluntary** is peculiar to English organ music. It is thought to have originated as a freely composed or improvised piece of music played by the organist during the church service. Voluntaries vary considerably in style. They may be based on a hymn tune or other melody, and they can have one or more movements.

There are many **concertos** written for the organ. Usually the organ is accompanied by an orchestra, as with other concertos, though there are many solo passages for the organ during the composition. The organ concerto, like most concertos, usually has three movements.

Much other music has been arranged for the organ, especially when the organ was being used as a substitute for an orchestra. The **orchestral transcription** was especially popular in the nineteenth century. Excerpts from operas, symphonies and other instrumental and vocal pieces were all arranged for organ solo. It was not uncommon, when the town-hall or concert-hall organ was popular, for recitals to consist solely of transcriptions of such compositions as 'The Ride of the Valkyries' from Wagner's Ring cycle!

Composers

Only the major composers are mentioned here. The bibliography gives details of other books which include information about organ music and organ composers.

Johann Sebastian Bach (1685-1750) is often thought of as the first great composer of organ music. However, the organ had already been in existence for several hundred years before he was born and there were many fine organists and writers of organ music working in earlier centuries. Some of the earliest organ music was also designed to be

Jan Sweelinck: 'Fantasia in Echo'. The organ is capable of sharp contrasts, especially loud stops on one manual and soft stops on another. This facility has been used to good effect by composers, as shown in this early example by Sweelinck.

played on other keyboard instruments — partly because an organ might not be available, partly because there was less of a distinction between different kinds of musical writing and partly because it would make the compositions more attractive to a larger number of potential players. English organ music, which was for manuals only until the early nineteenth century, was often labelled 'for organ or harpsichord' so that it would sell more easily. Some twentieth-century composers wrote their music for either organ or harmonium for similar reasons.

The best known early composers of keyboard and organ music include **Jan Sweelinck** (1562-1621), organist of the Oude Kerk, Amsterdam; **Jehan Titelouze** (1563-1633), organist of Rouen Cathedral; **Michael Praetorius** (1571-1621), German organist and writer on music and the organ; **Girolamo Frescobaldi** (1583-1643), organist of St Peter's Church, Rome; **Samuel Scheidt** (1587-1654), German organist and a pupil of Sweelinck; and **Johann Jakob Froberger** (1610-67), a Frenchman who worked in Austria and Italy and studied with Frescobaldi, as well as travelling elsewhere in Europe.

Works by these organ composers are still played regularly and form a major part of the repertoire. Each composer contributed to the development of one or more of the musical forms described earlier in this chapter. Sweelinck, for instance, is remembered for his fantasias (including the 'Echo' Fantasia, which uses loud and soft stops on different manuals to produce echoes), toccatas and variations. His best known work is probably the Variations on the popular song 'Mein junges Leben hat ein End' ('My young life hath an end'). This is a series of embellishments on the same melody, beginning and ending with simple variations, with more complex and virtuosic variations in between. Such music would be played while people walked round the church talking to each other.

Frescobaldi's music for the Catholic Church would be played before, during or after the service. He was famous, like Sweelinck, for his virtuoso and expressive playing and is particularly remembered for his toccatas. Titelouze wrote many organ hymns and magnificats (pieces based on the magnificat plainsong melodies). Praetorius composed in a wide range of styles and forms, as did Scheidt and Froberger.

English organ composers during the sixteenth and seventeenth centuries composed for smaller instruments, which were unlikely to have had pedals, and so the music could also be performed on other keyboard instruments. One of the most famous keyboard composers of his day was **John Bull** (1562-1628). After a period as organist of Hereford Cathedral and the Chapel Royal, London, he moved to Brussels as organist of the Royal Chapel and then to Antwerp, where he became organist at the cathedral. He was a close friend of Sweelinck and the two men obviously influenced each other in their compositions.

Sweelinck was a major influence on the development of organ playing and organ composition, having a number of pupils who became famous players and

The Organ

Jan Sweelinck: Variations on 'Mein junges Leben hat ein End'. Some organ music — and especially compositions not written for a particular religious setting — is based on popular tunes, as in this example. This is a set of variations on the same tune. Each variation arranges the melody in a different way. Note for instance the difference between variations 1 and 5. In variation 5 the harmony remains the same as in variation 1; the melody is embellished considerably, however. The dynamic and speed markings are modern, as are the instructions to use particular manuals (Rp = Rückpositiv; Hw = Hauptwerk).

composers in their own right. By the end of the seventeenth century, just as individual styles or schools of organ building were developing, so groups of organ composers, with different approaches and styles, were developing in each major country.

As the most highly developed instruments were built in Germany and Scandinavia, the major school of organ composition, which still forms the basis of the organist's repertoire, developed in these areas. **Dietrich Buxtehude** (1637-1707) was of Danish origin, though he spent most of his working life as organist in Lübeck, Germany. He wrote much orchestral and choral music as well as an extensive range of compositions for the organ consisting of toccatas, preludes, fantasias and fugues, chaconnes and a large number of chorale preludes.

Johann Sebastian Bach (1685-1750) greatly admired Buxtehude's playing and music and walked many miles from his home to Lübeck to hear him. Bach might have succeeded Buxtehude as organist at Lübeck, but he was not successful in the final competition for the post. It is said that he would have had to marry Buxtehude's daughter as part of the contract!

Bach's life was spent as organist, music director and composer to a number of churches and ducal courts in Germany. From 1723 until his death he was Kantor at St Thomas's Church, Leipzig, where much of his church music was composed. He came from a large musical family and was part of the German organist-composer tradition. He had over twenty children, many of whom were fine musicians and composers in their own right. Bach is regarded as the greatest composer of organ music and one of the greatest composers of any music of any period.

Over two hundred organ compositions written in a wide variety of styles form the backbone of the organist's repertoire. Bach wrote the best known organ piece of all, the Toccata and Fugue in D minor. It is generally regarded as an early work, though with its dramatic opening and sharp contrasts, its virtuoso fugue and final climax it is easy to understand why it has always been popular. This piece is one of a group of large-scale compositions which link an introductory toccata, fantasia, prelude or similar movement with a substantial fugue. The music is obviously intended to be played on a large instrument in a big building.

The chorale preludes and pieces based on hymn tunes are more reflective in style. The *Orgelbüchlein* ('Little Organ Book'), though not completed, contains chorale preludes for all parts of the church's year. Some of the other chorale preludes are less well known, though equally magnificent; the *Clavierübung* Part III is a collection of chorale preludes and settings of parts of the plainsong mass with a great Prelude at the start and the well known 'St Anne' Fugue (so called because the fugue melody is like the opening of the hymn tune 'St Anne' — 'O God our help in ages past') at the end. *Clavierübung* means literally 'key-

board practice' and the other parts of this great anthology contain music for harpsichord or other instruments. Volume III is devoted almost entirely to organ music and the technique of the organist is certainly tested in playing them. The six Schübler Chorale Preludes are named after their publisher and are mainly arrangements for organ of movements from Bach's choral cantatas, including the well known movement from 'Wachet auf, ruft uns die Stimme!' Bach was an avid student of music other than his own and he arranged (and often improved) compositions and based some of his works on their themes. A number of Antonio Vivaldi's string concertos survive in arrangements by Bach for organ.

As Bach was an organ teacher some of his organ music, for example the *Clavierübung*, was at least partly written as 'practice music' for his pupils. The trio sonatas, too, were designed to develop the player's independence of hands and feet. Some of the music was probably played on a pedal harpsichord as well as or instead of an organ and is chamber rather than church music. When organs were hand-blown it would be much easier and more comfortable to practise at home on a harpsichord!

Many of Bach's contemporaries also wrote music which is still played. **Johann Pachelbel** (1653-1706) held a number of important posts including that of organist of St Stephen's Cathedral in Vienna. **Vincent Lübeck** (1654-1706), **Georg Böhm** (1661-1733), **Nikolaus Bruhns** (1665-97), **Johann Gottfried Walther** (1684-1748) and **Johann Ludwig Krebs** (1713-80) all

The Organ

composed organ music which is familiar today.

Very different traditions of organ composition were developing in France and England during the eighteenth century. The French organ relied less on the pedals and more on the reed stops. The stop registration became very stylised — if not standardised — and the music reflects this. The organ mass was linked directly to the use of the instrument in the liturgy. More frivolous pieces, based on dance movements for example, were also composed, though these would be played on chamber rather than church organs. The main composers in a strong native tradition were **François Couperin** (1668-1733), organist to the king and one

of a family of musicians; **Nicolas de Grigny** (1671-1703), of Rheims; **Louis Nicolas Clérambault** (1676-1738), of Paris; and **Jean François d'Andrieu** (1682-1738), also of Paris. Many of their pieces were published in anthologies, such as Clérambault's *Livre d'Orgue* and d'Andrieu's *Pièces d'Orgue*. Couperin wrote and published two large-scale organ masses, one for parish churches (*Messe pour les Paroisses*) and one for monasteries (*Messe pour les Couvents*). Couperin corresponded extensively with Bach, some of whose music was undoubtedly influenced by the French composer; in particular, some of the rhythms used in French organ music (such as the *notes inégales*) are also found

John Stanley: 'Voluntary in D minor'. English eighteenth-century organ music was much simpler than, for example, German music of the period. There was no pedal part, and the music relied on solo stops and contrasts between loud and soft manuals for the main effects, as in this voluntary.

in Bach's pieces, as for example the great Prelude in E flat which opens the *Clavierübung*.

There was less interest in organ composition in England than on the continent. After the Restoration of the Monarchy in 1660 organists were again appointed to church and cathedral posts and some organ music was composed. **John Blow** (1649-1708) and his pupil **Henry Purcell** (1659-95) were both in their turn organist of Westminster Abbey and composers of much organ music, especially voluntaries. Purcell's most famous organ piece is probably the Voluntary on the 'Old Hundredth' hymn tune. The major English organists of the eighteenth century all composed organ music, including: **William Croft** (1678-1727), also for a time organist of Westminster Abbey; **Maurice Greene** (1695-1755), organist of St Paul's Cathedral; **William Boyce** (1710-79), Master of the King's Music; **William Walond** (1725-70) of Oxford; and **John Stanley** (1713-86). Their work consisted mainly of voluntaries which would normally have two or more movements, using either solo stops (as for example Cornet or Trumpet) or Full Organ or the 'Diapasons'. Stanley was the most prolific and best known, and several sets of voluntaries were published in his lifetime. Although blind from birth, he was organist of the Temple Church in London, where he played the fine Bernhard Smith organ. Handel is reputed to have rushed to hear Stanley play his final voluntaries, so highly did he regard his playing.

George Frideric Handel (1685-1759) composed little organ music. The bulk of his output for the organ takes the form of concertos for organ and orchestra which were designed to be played as interludes between acts of his operas or oratorios. Small organs were installed in theatres and opera houses for this purpose. There were even pipe organs in the London pleasure gardens (such as Vauxhall) for the playing of such concertos. Many of these pieces were composed in such a hurry that Handel had time only to write out the orchestral parts, improvising the organ solos as he went along. Even today, many printed versions of the concertos have the instruction *Organo ad libitum* and nothing more in the score.

By the end of the eighteenth century the organ was not as popular an instrument as it had been. The orchestra was increasingly popular and, as the piano developed as a powerful and expressive solo instrument, fewer composers of the first rank were attracted to the organ. **Wolfgang Amadeus Mozart** (1756-91) wrote some music, ostensibly for musical clock with organ pipes, which may be played on larger church instruments. **Franz Joseph Haydn** (1732-1809) wrote only small-scale organ works, as did **Ludwig van Beethoven** (1770-1827).

In the nineteenth century much organ music was transcribed from orchestral or choral music. Among the few notable composers who wrote for the organ, **Felix Mendelssohn** (1809-47) composed six sonatas — all substantial works — as well as three preludes and fugues and a number of other small-scale pieces. Like many organ composers before and since, he was a virtuoso player and gave many recitals.

Some celebrated virtuosos composed

The Organ

Franz Liszt: 'Fantasia and Fugue on BACH'. Nineteenth-century organ music required larger, more powerful instruments which could give a broad range of dynamics and timbres. The end of this virtuoso piece by Liszt shows the extremes needed, all within the space of ten bars. The music is much more chordal than contrapuntal and employs rapid harmonic changes, such as the change from G flat major to B major in the space of the first three bars of the example.

a small number of pieces for the organ. **Franz Liszt** (1811-86), the great Hungarian piano virtuoso, wrote mammoth compositions for the organ which demonstrated both the player's virtuosity and the power and dynamic range of the large organs on which the pieces had to be played. The most famous of these compositions is the Fantasia and Fugue on BACH (the note B in Germany is actually B flat; the note H is B natural). With its virtuoso keyboard writing, the piece taxes the technique of any player!

Julius Reubke (1834-58) looked set to emulate Liszt with his massive Sonata on the 94th Psalm. He died young and

this piece was his only major composition, though it remains a significant contribution to the repertoire.

Robert Schumann (1810-56) also wrote six fugues on the name of Bach as well as four sketches for pedal piano (a piano whose lower notes were activated also by an organ pedal board — a useful practice instrument, like the pedal harpsichord). **Johannes Brahms** (1833-97) also wrote organ pieces, including thirteen delightful miniatures based on chorale tunes. Probably the best known is 'Es ist ein Ros' entsprungen' ('A beautiful rose has blossomed').

The most prolific German organ composers, all themselves regular players were **Josef Rheinberger** (1840-1901), **Max Reger** (1873-1916) and **Sigfried Karg-Elert** (1877-1935). Rheinberger is chiefly remembered for his twenty organ sonatas, which are now enjoying a revival in popularity. He was a prolific composer of all kinds of music and his organ repertoire is varied, including preludes, fantasias, toccatas and fugues as well as much chorale-based writing. It is notable for its complexity, being written for the heavy German organs of the late nineteenth and early twentieth centuries. Karg-Elert based much of his music on chorales, and his Improvisations are still popular in the repertoire.

As a result of the Cavaillé-Coll organ and the work of organ tutors at the Paris Conservatoire, a substantial school of organ composition developed in France in the nineteenth century and continued in the twentieth. Though his own output was small, **César Franck** (1822-90) had a significant influence on French organists and organ composers through his distinctive style, as evinced by the Six Pieces and the Three Chorals, his last work. **Charles-Marie Widor** (1845-1937), famous for the Toccata from his Fifth Organ Symphony, wrote much organ music, including nine organ symphonies.

Much exciting and often difficult music has been written for the organ by French composers. Organists writing in the twentieth century have included **Jean Langlais, Charles Tournemire, Joseph Jongen, Jehan Alain** and **Olivier Messiaen**. Tournemire wrote some 51 organ masses. Alain was killed while still young, but his well known piece 'Litanies' shows what a great composer he would have been. Messiaen is perhaps the greatest organ composer of the twentieth century. His organ pieces indicate his highly religious background

Johannes Brahms: 'Es ist ein Ros' entsprungen'. Some nineteenth-century organ music was modelled on the earlier chorale prelude, as in this short and simple example by Brahms. The music is chordal, like some of Bach's simpler preludes, and the melody is in the upper part of the right hand, where it is embellished.

The Organ

combined with an interest in bird song and non-western tonalities and a highly individual rhythmic structure. Many of his compositions centre upon the church's calendar and scenes from the life of Christ, for example, *La Nativité* and *L'Ascension*.

No other European school of organ composition compares with that in France in the late nineteenth and twentieth centuries. Most of the great twentieth century composers such as Britten, Tippett, Stravinsky and Shostakovich have either not written music for the organ or produced only a handful of compositions. Other famous composers have begun their careers as organists and church musicians but have left little organ music. Edward Elgar is a good example. Though a church organist, he composed only one piece for the organ, the Sonata in G. There are many organ composers from England, Germany, Scandinavia and, increasingly, North America, but none has yet achieved the stature of either Messiaen or the great writers of organ music of previous centuries.

There is a rich catalogue of music for the instrument which can regularly be heard in churches and concert halls, at services, recitals and concerts. Though the organ is primarily a solo or an accompanimental instrument, there are also concertos by composers of every age which are regularly played. At the highest professional levels of organ playing, standards of performance have never been better, as a result of the thorough training available at colleges and universities in Britain, Europe and North America. While there is a shortage of people willing to play the church organ in many places, competition for organ scholarships and concert engagements is fierce. Being an organist — at whatever level of competence — is not easy and the organ student must devote many hours to practice and study of the instrument and its construction. Once mastered, however, the organ is rewarding to play. It is equally satisfying to listen to good organs and well played organ music. Modern recording techniques have ensured that high-quality performances on historic organs from many countries are readily available to anyone interested in the instrument and its music.

No other instrument has the same dynamic range, the same multiplicity of colours, the same rich and varied heritage as the organ. No other instrument has such a complex mechanism. No other instrument stretches the mind and body of the player in the way that the organ does. It is a unique instrument which continues to fascinate and excite many people, whether as players or listeners. It is truly the King of Instruments.

End-note

In most areas there is an association or club for those interested in the organ and its music. There are also specialist societies for devotees of the fairground organ, the cinema organ and the barrel organ. The local public library service should be able to provide their addresses.

4
Gazetteer

This gazetteer lists a number of organs in the United Kingdom which are worth visiting, either because they are of historic importance, or because they are major examples of individual builders' work, or because they represent the best of a particular style of organ building.

Appleby, Cumbria: St Lawrence. Anonymous seventeenth-century case and some pipes moved from Carlisle Cathedral in 1684.

Armitage, Staffordshire: Parish Church. Case and some pipes from the 1790 organ by Samuel Green, originally built for Lichfield Cathedral.

Barnard Castle, County Durham: The Bowes Museum, Barnard Castle DL12 8NP. Telephone: 0833 690606. Includes several barrel organs in its collection of musical instruments.

Bath, Avon: Abbey. Four-manual organ originally built by William Hill, 1868.

Belfast, Northern Ireland: Ulster Hall. Four-manual organ by William Hill, 1861, 1903. Restored by Noel Mander, 1978. Widely regarded as Hill's finest instrument.

Beverley, Humberside: Minster. Large four-manual organ by Hill, 1884, 1916, incorporating much of the original pipework from the Snetzler organ of 1769.

Birmingham, West Midlands: Cathedral. Case by Thomas Schwarbrick, 1715.

Birmingham, West Midlands: Town Hall. Five-manual organ by Noel Mander, based on the William Hill organ of 1834, with additions in 1843, 1890 and 1933.

Blackburn, Lancashire: Cathedral. Large three-manual organ by J. W. Walker, 1969, in open, caseless position.

Blair Atholl, Tayside: Blair Castle, Blair Atholl, Pitlochry, Perthshire PH18 5TL. Telephone: 0796 481207. Positive-regal by John Loosemore, 1650.

Blandford Forum, Dorset: St Peter and St Paul. Three-manual organ by George Pike England, 1794; rebuilt Hill, 1876; restored Noel Mander, 1971.

Brentford, Middlesex: The Musical Museum, 368 High Street, Brentford, Middlesex TW8 0BD. Telephone: 081-560 8108. Includes a Wurlitzer organ originally built for the Regal Theatre, Kingston upon Thames.

Bristol, Avon: Anglican Cathedral. Four-manual organ originally built by Renatus Harris, 1685; rebuilt by J. W. Walker, 1907. Harris's original main case survives, though somewhat altered.

Bristol, Avon: Roman Catholic Cathedral. Modern three-manual classical organ built by Rieger of Austria.

Bristol, Avon: St Mary Redcliffe Church. Large four-manual organ by Harrison and Harrison, originally built 1912 and widely regarded as amongst the firm's finest instruments.

Bury St Edmunds, Suffolk: Moyse's Hall Museum, Cornhill, Bury St Edmunds IP33 1DZ. Telephone: 0284 757063 or 757072. Includes a chamber organ.

Cambridge: Christ's College. Early eighteenth-century organ case and some pipes, possibly built by Bernhard Smith; restored 1983.

Cambridge: Jesus College. Small organ by Bishop, 1849, based on Bernhard Smith pipes. Large organ by Noel Mander, 1971.

Cambridge: King's College. Main case by Dallam, 1606; Chair case by Pease, 1661. Four-manual organ by Harrison and Harrison, 1934; revised 1968.

Cambridge: Pembroke College. Two-manual organ consisting of Great, Chair and Pedal, built by Noel Mander in 1980 and based on early eighteenth-century pipework and case.

Cambridge: Peterhouse. Three-manual Snetzler organ and case, 1765; restored and rebuilt, Noel Mander, 1963.

Cambridge: St John's College. Large four-manual organ by Hill, Norman and Beard, 1955.

Cambridge: St Mary's University Church. Largely original Bernhard Smith three-manual organ and case, 1698; rebuilt 1870; restored 1963.

Cambridge: Trinity College. Three-manual organ by Metzler of Zürich, 1976, using main and Chair cases of the Bernhard Smith organ of 1708, together with a few original pipes.

Canterbury, Kent: Cathedral. Three-manual 'Father' Willis, 1886; rebuilt Noel Mander, 1979-80. This was one of Willis's first instruments to use electro-pneumatic action and includes a 'nave' section.

Cardiff, South Glamorgan: Llandaff Cathedral. Four-manual organ by Hill, Norman and Beard, 1938, 1958, based on an instrument built by Robert Hope-Jones, 1898.

Carisbrooke, Isle of Wight: Carisbrooke Castle Museum, Carisbrooke, Newport PO30 1XY. Telephone: 0983 523112. Three-stop chamber organ built by Hoffheimer, c.1602. Thought to be of Flemish origin and built for John Graham, Earl of Montrose. Played by Princess Elizabeth, daughter of Charles I, while in captivity at Carisbrooke.

Cheltenham, Gloucestershire: Cheltenham Art Gallery and Museum, Clarence Street, Cheltenham GL50 3JT. Telephone: 0242 237431. Musical instrument collection includes two small organs.

Chester, Cheshire: Cathedral. Large four-manual organ by Whiteley, 1876; Hill, 1910; conservatively rebuilt, 1970.

Chichester, West Sussex: Cathedral. Organ largely by William Hill, 1851, 1859 and 1888, but based on earlier work by Harris, 1678, and Byfield, 1725, and restored by Noel Mander in 1985. Includes a 'nave' section.

Cotton, Suffolk: Mechanical Music Museum, Blacksmith's Road, Cotton, Stowmarket IP14 4QN. Telephone: 0449 781354, 781988 or 613876. Includes a large Mortier café organ and a Wurlitzer theatre organ originally in Leicester Square Theatre, London.

Coventry, West Midlands: Cathedral.

Modern four-manual organ similar in design to the organ of the Royal Festival Hall, London, by Harrison and Harrison, 1962.

Doncaster, South Yorkshire: Parish Church. Five-manual organ by Schulze, 1862; rebuilt J. W. Walker, 1935.

Douglas, Isle of Man: Manx Museum and National Trust, Douglas. Telephone: 0624 675522. Collection includes two barrel organs.

Downpatrick, Northern Ireland: Down Cathedral. Eighteenth-century case and possibly pipework.

Durham: Cathedral. Large four-manual organ by Harrison and Harrison, 1905, 1935, 1970, incorporating pipework by Willis. Parts of the case of the original Bernhard Smith organ of 1683-4 survive.

Edinburgh, Lothian: Russell Collection of Harpsichords and Clavichords, St Cecilia's Hall, Niddry Street, Cowgate, Edinburgh. Telephone: 031-650 2805. Collection includes several small organs.

Edinburgh, Lothian: University School of Music. Two-manual Werkprinzip organ by Ahrend of Denmark, 1978.

Ellesmere, Shropshire: Ellesmere College Great Hall. Three-manual organ by Schulze, originally built for St Mary's Church, Tyne Dock, 1864, 1874.

Ely, Cambridgeshire: Cathedral. Large four-manual Harrison and Harrison organ, 1908; rebuilt 1975. Widely regarded as the definitive Harrison organ. Case by Gilbert Scott, 1851, based on medieval Gothic examples.

Eton, Berkshire: Eton College. The Chapel contains a large four-manual organ by Hill, 1882, 1902, rebuilt with tubular-pneumatic action by Noel Mander. The Memorial Hall contains main and Chair cases and some pipes from the Mittenreiter organ built in 1773 for the English Church in Rotterdam, rebuilt in 1973 by Flentrop of Zaandam, Holland.

Exeter, Devon: Cathedral. Great and Chair cases of John Loosemore organ of 1665. Present instrument by Willis, 1891; Harrison and Harrison, 1936 and 1965.

Finedon, Northamptonshire: St Mary's Church. Three-manual organ by Christopher Shrider, 1717, largely unaltered. Shrider was Bernhard Smith's son-in-law.

Framlingham, Suffolk: St Michael's Church. Two-manual organ by Thomas Thamar, 1674, originally built for Pembroke College, Cambridge. The case is reputed to be older still.

Glasgow, Strathclyde: Glasgow Art Gallery and Museum, Kelvingrove, Glasgow G3 8AG. Telephone: 041-357 3929. Home of the Kelvingrove organ built by T. C. Lewis in 1901 and restored 1987-8.

Gloucester: Cathedral. Four-manual organ by Hill, Norman and Beard, 1971, incorporating pipes from the original Harris organ of 1665 and the original main and Chair cases.

Goudhurst, Kent: Finchcocks Living Museum of Music, Goudhurst TN17 1HH. Telephone: 0580 211702. Includes several chamber and barrel organs.

Great Packington, Warwickshire: St James's Church. Organ by Richard

Bridge, designed by Handel.

Halifax, West Yorkshire: Parish Church. Four-manual Harrison and Harrison organ, 1929, incorporating some pipes from the Snetzler organ of 1766.

Hexham, Northumberland: Abbey. Large two-manual organ by Lawrence Phelps, modelled on the French classical organ.

Hillsborough, Northern Ireland: Parish Church. Case and much pipework by Snetzler, 1773.

Huddersfield, West Yorkshire: St Paul's Hall, Huddersfield Polytechnic. Three-manual Werkprinzip organ by Wood of Huddersfield, 1977.

Huddersfield, West Yorkshire: Town Hall. Four-manual organ by Willis, 1881, restored Harrison and Harrison, 1981.

Hull, Humberside: Holy Trinity Church. Large four-manual organ by Compton, based on the Forster and Andrews instrument of 1876, 1908.

Kilmarnock, Strathclyde: Dean Castle, Dean Road, Kilmarnock, Ayrshire. Telephone: 0563 34580. Musical instrument collection includes several early small organs.

King's Lynn, Norfolk: St Margaret's Church. The case and some pipes from Snetzler's large three-manual organ of 1754 remain.

Leeds, West Yorkshire: Parish Church. Large four-manual organ in Victorian Gothic case with no pipes.

Leeds, West Yorkshire: St Bartholomew's Church, Armley. Four-manual organ by Schulze, 1869.

Leeds, West Yorkshire: Town Hall. Three-manual organ by Wood, Wordsworth of Leeds, 1971, based on a five-manual instrument by Gray and Davison, 1859, 1865.

Leicester: Cathedral. Four-manual organ by Harrison and Harrison, 1930, incorporating pipework from the Snetzler organ of 1774.

Lichfield, Staffordshire: Cathedral. Four-manual organ by Hill, 1884, 1908; rebuilt 1973, but based on an instrument built in 1861 by G. M. Holdich. At the time it was first constructed, this organ had one of the most complete Pedal divisions of any cathedral organ in Britain.

Lincoln: Cathedral. Last cathedral organ built by 'Father' Willis, 1898. Conservatively rebuilt and restored, 1960, by Harrison and Harrison.

Liskeard, Cornwall: Paul Corin's Magnificent Music Machines, St Keyne Station, Liskeard PL14 4SH. Telephone: 0579 343108. The collection includes several mechanical organs and the 1929 Wurlitzer organ previously in the Regent Theatre, Brighton.

Little Bardfield, Essex: St Katherine's Church. Case by Renatus Harris (?), 1689.

Little Walsingham, Norfolk: St Mary's Church. Two-manual organ by Cedric Arnold Williamson and Hyatt. An early British classical organ.

Liverpool, Merseyside: Anglican Cathedral. Five-manual organ by Willis, 1923-6, 1960-5; rebuilt Harrison and Harrison, 1977. The largest pipe organ in Britain. There is also a two-manual organ in the Cathedral's Lady Chapel.

Liverpool, Merseyside: Liverpool Museum, William Brown Street, Liverpool L3 8EN. Telephone: 051-207 0001. Includes a portative organ by

Nicolaus Wandersheid, Nuremberg, 1644, a 1767 Snetzler chamber organ, a 'bottle' organ and a barrel organ.

Liverpool, Merseyside: Roman Catholic Cathedral. Large four-manual organ by J. W. Walker, 1967.

Liverpool, Merseyside: St George's Hall. Large four-manual concert organ by Willis, 1854-5, 1897, 1931.

London: The British Museum, Great Russell Street, London WC18 3DG. Telephone: 071-636 1555. The musical instrument collections contain early Pan-pipes.

London: Christ Church, Spitalfields. Large three-manual organ and case by Richard Bridge, 1730. Largely unaltered, though not now playable.

London: The Iveagh Bequest, Kenwood, Hampstead Lane, London NW3 7JR. Telephone: 081-348 1286. Includes a chamber organ by John England, c.1790.

London: N. P. Mander Limited, Tower Hamlets, St Peter's Organ Works, London E2 7AF. A small collection of chamber and table organs.

London: Royal Albert Hall, Kensington. Large four-manual organ (111 stops) by Harrison and Harrison, 1926, based on the 1871 organ by 'Father' Willis.

London: Royal College of Music Museum of Instruments, Prince Consort Road, South Kensington, London SW7 2BS. Telephone: 071-589 3643. Collection includes a table regal, c.1629, and a chamber organ possibly by Bernhard Smith, 1702.

London: Royal Festival Hall, South Bank. Caseless four-manual organ by Harrison and Harrison, 1954. The first large British organ to return to a classical specification and methods of voicing.

London: Royal Naval College, Greenwich. Three-manual organ and case originally by Samuel Green, 1789.

London: St Anne, Limehouse. Three-manual organ built originally for the Great Exhibition of 1851 by Gray and Davison.

London: St Botolph, Aldgate. Two-manual organ by Noel Mander, based on the case and pipes of a Renatus Harris instrument of the 1670s.

London: St Bride, Fleet Street. Large four-manual extension organ by Compton, 1958.

London: St Giles, Camberwell. Large, almost untouched three-manual organ by J. C. Bishop, 1844.

London: St Giles, Cripplegate. Three-manual organ by Noel Mander based on a case and pipes by Jordan and Bridge, 1733.

London: St James, Clerkenwell. Two-manual organ and case by George Pike England, 1792; restored by Noel Mander, 1978.

London: St Leonard, Shoreditch. Organ case by Bridge, 1754.

London: St Magnus the Martyr, London Bridge. Case of 1712 organ by Abraham Jordan, reputed to contain the first swell box in Britain.

London: St Mary, Rotherhithe. Three-manual organ by Byfield, 1764, largely unaltered.

London: St Mary-at-Hill. Three-manual organ by William Hill, 1848, 1879, largely unaltered.

London: St Mary Magdalene, Holloway Road. Organ by George Pike England, 1814, rebuilt by 'Father' Willis in 1867.

The Organ

The organ in the church of St Andrew, Holborn, London, 1989. Note the conveyancing pipes inside the case immediately behind the feet of the large front pipes.

Gazetteer

Willis was organist of the church for over thirty years.

London: St Paul's Cathedral. Five-manual organ by Mander, 1977, based on the 'Father' Willis organ of 1872. Cases from the original Bernhard Smith organ of 1697, designed by Sir Christopher Wren. Includes a 'nave' section.

London: St Peter, Cornhill. Three-manual organ with case and some pipes by Bernhard Smith, 1681.

London: St Vedast, Foster Lane. Three-manual organ originally by Harris and Byfield.

London: Southwark Cathedral. Four-manual organ originally built by T. C. Lewis, in the style of Schulze, 1896.

London: Temple Church. Large four-manual Harrison and Harrison, 1927/1954, originally built for the ballroom of Glentanar Castle, Scotland.

London: Victoria and Albert Museum, Cromwell Road, South Kensington, London SW7 2RL. Telephone: 071-938 8500. Includes a combined harpsichord and organ of 1579.

London: Westminster Abbey. Five-manual organ by Harrison and Harrison, originally built 1937. Cases by J. L. Pearson, 1899.

London: Westminster Roman Catholic Cathedral. Large four-manual organ by Willis, 1922-32, restored Harrison and Harrison, 1984.

Ludlow, Shropshire: Parish Church. Case and some pipes from the original Snetzler organ of 1764.

Lulworth, Dorset: Lulworth Castle. Large one-manual organ by Brice Seede, 1785.

Macclesfield, Cheshire: Adlington Hall, near Macclesfield SK10 4LF. Telephone: 0625 829206. Anonymous two-manual organ. The largest surviving seventeenth-century organ in Britain.

Manchester: Royal Northern College of Music. Large three-manual classical organ by Hradetzky, 1973. The Watson Collection includes a barrel organ.

Napton-on-the-Hill, Warwickshire: Napton Nickelodeon of Mechanical Music, Napton-on-the-Hill, near Rugby. Collection includes various barrel organs and the Compton cinema organ originally built for the Hammersmith Regal.

Newcastle upon Tyne, Tyne and Wear: Cathedral. Four-manual organ by Nicholson, 1981, incorporating a case by Renatus Harris, 1676.

Northleach, Gloucestershire: Keith Harding's World of Mechanical Music, High Street, Northleach GL54 3EU. Telephone: 0451 860181. Includes a barrel organ and other mechanical 'organs'.

Norwich, Norfolk: Cathedral. Large four-manual by Hill, Norman and Beard, 1940-1, 1968-70. The second largest cathedral organ in Britain.

Norwich, Norfolk: The Old Meeting House, Colegate. Case and some pipes from a seventeenth-century organ, possibly by Robert Dallam.

Norwich, Norfolk: St George, Colegate. Two-manual organ by George Pike England, 1802.

Norwich, Norfolk: St Peter Hungate Church Museum, Princes Street, Norwich NR3 1AE. Telephone: 0603 667231. Includes a barrel organ c.1820 and an Italian positive organ of *c.*1625.

Norwich, Norfolk: St Peter Mancroft Church. Large three-manual Werkprinzip organ by Peter Collins, 1984.

Nottingham: Albert Hall. Large four-manual organ by J. J. Binns, in the style of Schulze, 1901.

Nottingham: St Mary's Parish Church. Two-manual classical organ, complete with Brustwerk folding doors by Marcussen of Denmark, 1973. A smaller instrument, by the same builder, can be found in St Mary's Clifton, Nottingham.

Old Bilton, Warwickshire: St Mark. Case by Dallam, 1636.

Old Radnor, Powys: St Stephen's Church. Anonymous sixteenth-century case.

Oundle, Northamptonshire: Oundle School. Modern Werkprinzip organ by Frobenius of Copenhagen, 1984.

Oxford: Christ Church Cathedral. Four-manual classical organ by Rieger, 1979, but housed in Bernhard Smith's original case.

Oxford: Magdalen College. Two-manual organ by Noel Mander. The Great organ is in the 'Chair' position, in a stone case on the chapel screen.

Oxford: New College. Large three-manual Werkprinzip organ by Grant, Degens and Bradbeer, 1969.

Oxford: Queen's College. Two-manual organ by Frobenius of Copenhagen. One of the first Werkprinzip organs in Britain.

Paisley, Strathclyde: Abbey. Four-manual organ by J. W. Walker, 1968, with pipework from the organ by Cavaillé-Coll, 1872.

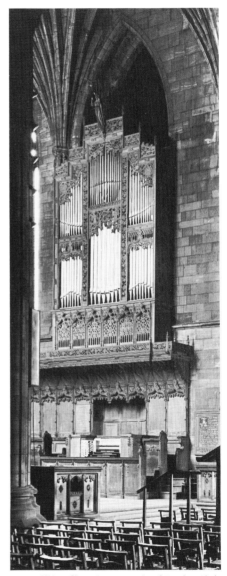

Cavaillé-Coll et Compagnie of Paris originally built the four-manual organ at Paisley Abbey, Strathclyde, in 1872, but it was rebuilt in 1968 by J. W. Walker and Sons. It has 66 stops and electric action.

Gazetteer

Peterborough, Cambridgeshire: Cathedral. Large four-manual organ by Hill, originally built 1894 and little altered since.

Portsea, Hampshire: St Mary's Church. Large three-manual organ by J. W. Walker, 1891.

Preston, Lancashire: St George the Martyr's Church. Three-manual 'Father' Willis organ, 1865, largely unaltered.

Ripon, North Yorkshire: Minster. Four-manual organ by Harrison and Harrison, 1913, 1926, 1963, incorporating pipework by Lewis and Renn and a case by Gilbert Scott of 1878.

Romsey, Hampshire: Abbey. Large three-manual organ by J. W. Walker, 1848, 1888.

Rotherham, South Yorkshire: Parish Church. Present instrument incorporates parts of the original Snetzler instrument of 1777.

Rugby, Warwickshire: Brownsover Church. Case possibly by Dallam, 1661.

St Albans, Hertfordshire: Abbey. Large three-manual organ by Harrison and Harrison, 1962.

St Albans, Hertfordshire: St Albans Organ Museum, 320 Camp Road, St Albans. Telephone: 0727 51557. Includes several fairground organs and two cinema organs, one a Wurlitzer built originally for the Granada, Edmonton, in 1933, the other built by Spurden Rutt for the Regal, Highams Park.

St Andrews, Fife: University Church. Four-manual organ by Hradetzky, 1974.

Salford, Manchester: St Paul's Church. Two-manual organ by Samuel Green, 1787, largely unaltered.

Salford, Manchester: St Philip's Church. Two-manual organ by Renn and Boston, 1829, largely unaltered.

Salisbury, Wiltshire: Cathedral. Four-manual organ by 'Father' Willis, 1876. Reputed to be his best cathedral organ.

Salisbury, Wiltshire: St Thomas's Church. Organ originally by Samuel Green, 1792, built for the cathedral.

Saltaire, West Yorkshire: Museum of Victorian Reed Organs and Harmoniums, Victoria Hall, Victoria Road, Saltaire, Shipley. Telephone (after 5 pm): 0274 585601. The only museum of its kind in Europe.

Selby, North Yorkshire: Abbey. Large four-manual organ originally built by Hill, 1909.

Sherborne, Dorset: Abbey. Large three-manual organ originally built by Gray and Davison, 1856.

Stanford-on-Avon, Northamptonshire: St Nicholas's Church. Early organ case (1580s) on west gallery.

Staunton Harold, Leicestershire: Private Chapel. Contains a small organ reputed to be the work of Bernhard Smith.

Tewkesbury, Gloucestershire: Abbey. Choir organ incorporates the case and front pipes from an organ probably built by Robert Dallam for Magdalen College, Oxford, in 1637. Four-manual North Transept organ originally built by Michell and Thynne for the Inventions Exhibition of 1885. Their magnum opus, the organ is one of the high-points of the British romantic organ movement.

Thaxted, Essex: Parish Church. Large

three-manual by Henry Lincoln, 1826, largely untouched. Small organ has case supposedly by George Pike England.

Thursford, Norfolk: The Thursford Collection, Thursford Green, Thursford, Fakenham NR21 0AS. Telephone: 0328 878477. Contains several fairground or dance organs and a Wurlitzer theatre organ originally built for the Paramount Theatre, Leeds.

Truro, Cornwall: Cathedral. Almost untouched four-manual 'Father' Willis organ of 1888.

Twickenham, Middlesex: All Hallows' Church. Organ originally built by Renatus Harris, 1695.

Wakefield, West Yorkshire: Cathedral. Five-manual organ by Compton, partly built using the extension principle.

Warrington, Cheshire: Parr Hall. Organ built by Cavaillé-Coll, 1870.

Wells, Somerset: Cathedral. Four-manual Harrison and Harrison organ, 1910, 1973, based on an 1857 'Father' Willis instrument.

Whaplode St Catherine, Lincolnshire: Rutland Cottage Music Museum, Millgate, Whaplode St Catherine, Spalding. Telephone: 0406 540379. Includes church, chamber, barrel and reed organs, as well as an 'orgapian', a combined organ and piano for accompanying films.

Wigan, Lancashire: St Peter's Church, Hindley. Three-manual organ by Schulze, 1873.

Winchester, Hampshire: Cathedral. Large four-manual organ by Willis/Harrison and Harrison based on

'Father' Willis's organ for the Great Exhibition of 1851. Includes a 'nave' section.

Winchester, Hampshire: Winchester College Chapel. Large three-manual organ by Noel Mander, 1984, in case by W. D. Caroe, 1908.

Windsor, Berkshire: St George's Chapel, Windsor Castle. Large four-manual organ by Harrison and Harrison, 1965.

Wolverhampton, West Midlands: St John's. Case and some pipes by Renatus Harris, 1684.

Woodstock, Oxfordshire: Blenheim Palace, Woodstock OX7 1PX. Telephone: 0993 811325. Three-manual organ by 'Father' Willis, 1891, in the Long Library. The instrument can be played automatically as well as by an organist.

Worcester: Cathedral. Large four-manual organ by Harrison and Harrison, 1925, 1972, based on an instrument built by Robert Hope-Jones, 1896. The cathedral now also has a large electronic organ for the accompaniment of services in the nave.

Wymondham, Norfolk: Abbey. Large three-manual organ by James Davis, 1793. Rebuilt 1954, 1973. One-manual chamber organ also by Davis, 1810.

York: Minster. Large four-manual organ first built in 1829 by Elliot and Hill and originally the largest organ in Britain. Rebuilt at various times by J. W. Walker and Harrison and Harrison. The original Gothick case remains.

5
Further reading

There is a vast literature relating to the organ, its history and construction, its music and its players, as well as descriptions of individual instruments and histories of particular organ builders. The following list is a small selection of the main, easily accessible texts which give further information about the history and development of the instrument and its music. All the items listed contain further references to other, more detailed books and periodical articles.

There are several periodicals devoted to the organ. The two most general ones are *The Organ* and *The Organist's Review*. These are available through most music shops. *The Organist's Review* also gives details from time to time of the various clubs and organisations which organists and lovers of organ music can join. One of these is the British Institute for Organ Studies (BIOS), c/o Dr Christopher Kent, Department of Music, University of Reading, 35 Upper Redlands Road, Reading, Berkshire RG1 5JE, which aims to log historic instruments and to support their sympathetic restoration, as well as maintaining an archive of all important papers relating to organs and organ building in Britain.

Arnold, C.R. *Organ Literature: A Comprehensive Survey* (two volumes). Scarecrow Press, 1984.

Donahue, T. *Modern Classical Organ: A Guide to its Physical and Musical Structure.* McFarland, 1991.

Douglass, F. *The Language of the Classical French Organ: A Musical Tradition before 1800.* Yale University Press, 1969.

Edson, J.S. *Organ Preludes: An Index to Compositions on Hymn Tunes, Chorales, Plainsong Melodies, Gregorian Tunes and Carols* (two volumes). Scarecrow Press, 1970.

Hopkins, E.J., and Rimbault, E.F. *The Organ: Its History and Construction.* Frits Knuf, 1981 (reprint of 1877 edition). Includes specifications of many famous nineteenth-century organs.

Hurford, P. *Making Music on the Organ.* Oxford University Press, new edition, 1990. A comprehensive study of organ-playing technique and interpretation.

Landon, J.W. *Behold the Mighty Wurlitzer: History of the Theatre Pipe Organ.* Greenwood, 1983.

Langwill, L.G., and Boston, N. *Church and Chamber Barrel Organs.* Langwill, 1979.

Neal, R. *The Roy Neal Survey of Organ Registrations and Techniques.* Sceptre Publications, 1982.

Rowntree, J.P., and Brennan, J.F. *The Classical Organ in Britain* (three volumes). Positif Press, 1975-93. Specifications, line drawings and photographs of 'classical' organs built 1945 to 1990.

The Organ

Sumner, W.L. *The Organ: Its Evolution, Principles of Construction and Use.* MacDonald, 1952.

Thistlethwaite, N. *The Making of the Victorian Organ.* Cambridge University Press, 1990.

Williams, P. *The European Organ, 1450-1850.* Batsford, 1966. A detailed and comprehensive study.

Williams, P. *The Organ in Western Culture.* Cambridge University Press, 1993.

Williams, P. *A New History of the Organ: from the Greeks to the Present Day.* Faber, 1980.

Williams, P. *The Organ Music of J.S. Bach* (three volumes). Cambridge University Press, 1985-9. The definitive study of Bach's organ music.

Williams, P., and Owen, B. *The Organ* (The Grove Musical Instrument Series). Macmillan, 1988. Includes glossaries of stop names and organ-building terms and a list of major organ builders past and present.

Wills, A. *The Organ.* Kahn & Averill, second revised edition 1993.

Wilson, M.I. *Organ Cases of Western Europe.* C. Hurst, 1979.

Wilson, M.L. *The English Chamber Organ: History and Development, 1650-1850.* Cassirer, 1968.

Wyatt, G. *At the Mighty Organ.* Oxford Illustrated Press, 1974. History of cinema organ.

The five-manual organ console and case of St Paul's Cathedral, built by Mander, 1977, based on the 'Father' Willis organ of 1872. The cases are from the original Bernhard Smith organ of 1697, designed by Sir Christopher Wren. It includes a 'nave' section.

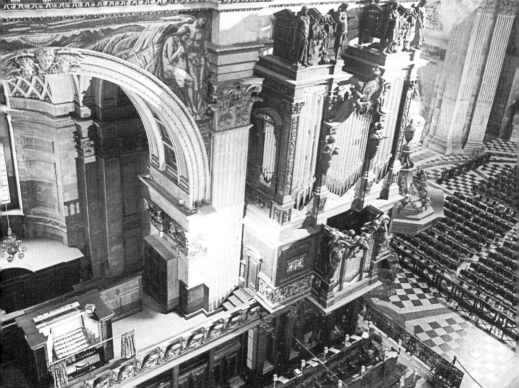

6
Discography
Compiled by Joan Welsby

The following list of recordings aims to provide a representative sample of currently available releases of organ music. The first sequence of recordings is arranged according to composer, the second according to artist. Recordings in this second list contain pieces by many different composers. Where known, the organs on which the music is played have been noted.

The name of the recording company is given, followed by the disc or cassette number. Where there are two numbers, the first refers to the compact disc recording and the second (in italics) to the cassette. When only one number is cited this refers to the compact disc recording unless printed in italics, in which case the recording is on cassette only.

Composers

Alain, Jehan. Thomas Trotter. *Organ Works*. Argo 430 833-2ZH.

Bach, C.P.E. Roland Munch/Hartmut Haenchen. Capriccio Digital 10 135; *CC 27 114*.

Bach, J.S. Marie-Claire Alain. *Organ Works*. Erato 2292-45054-2.

Marie-Claire Alain. Erato 2292-45188-2.

Marie-Claire Alain. Erato 2292-45190-2.

Marie-Claire Alain (organ of St Laurentskerk, Alkmaar). *Organ Works Volume 8*. Erato 4509-91702-2.

David Baker. *Baker Plays Bach*. Can be obtained from Wymondham Abbey shop.

Kevin Bowyer (organ of St Hans Kirche, Odense, Denmark). *Organ Works Volume 1*. Nimbus NI 5280.

Kevin Bowyer (organ of St Hans Kirche, Odense, Denmark). *Organ Works Volume 2*. Nimbus NI 5289.

Kevin Bowyer (organ of St Hans Kirche, Odense, Denmark). *Organ Works Volume 3*. Nimbus NI 5290.

Daniel Chorzempa. *Organ Works*. Philips 422 965-2PCC; *422 965-4PCC*.

Daniel Chorzempa. *Organ Recital*. Philips 432 610-2PM; *432 610-4PM*.

Lorenzo Ghielmi (organ of St Simpliciano, Milan). *Organ Works Volume 3*. Deutsche Harmonia Mundi 05472 772778-2.

Peter Hurford (organs of Ratzeburg Cathedral, Germany, and Church of Our Lady of Sorrows, Toronto, Canada). Argo 411 824-2; *411 824-4*.

Peter Hurford (various organs). Decca 417 711-2; *417 276-4*.

The Organ

Piet Kee (organ of St Bavo, Haarlem). Chandos 'Chaconne' CHAN 0527.

Ton Koopman (organ of Grote Keerk, Leeuwarden, Holland). Novalis Digital 150 036-2; *150 036-4*.

Ton Koopman (Christian Müller organ, Waalse-Kerk, Amsterdam, Holland). Novalis Digital 150 005-2; *150 005-4*.

Ton Koopman (Gabler organ of Weingarten Basilika, Germany). Novalis Digital 150 020-2; *150 020-4*.

Richard Marlow (Metzler organ of Trinity College, Cambridge). *Das Orgelbüchlein*. Mirabilis MRCD 904.

Michael Murray (organ of St Andreas-Kirche, Hildesheim, Germany). Telarc Digital CD 80127.

Michael Murray (organs at Congregational Church, Los Angeles, USA). Telarc CD 80088.

Michael Murray (organ at Methuen Memorial Hall, Massachusetts, USA). Telarc Digital CD 80049.

Jacques van Oortmersson (organ of Walloon Church, Amsterdam, Holland). Denon Digital C37 7376.

Hans Otto (Silbermann organ, Freiberg, Germany). Denon Digital C37 7004.

Joseph Payne. *Chorale Preludes*. Harmonia Mundi HMA 1909 5158.

Simon Preston. Deutsche Grammophon 427 668-2GH; *427 668-4GH*.

Simon Preston. Deutsche Grammophon 435 381-2GH.

Michael Radulescu (organ of St Simpliciano, Milan). *Organ Works Volume 2*. Deutsche Harmonia Mundi 05472 772762.

Lionel Rogg. EMI Eminence CD-EMX2 189; *TC-EMX2 189*.

Lionel Rogg. *Chorals de Noël*. Harmonia Mundi HMA190 717; *HMA43 717*.

Lionel Rogg. Harmonia Mundi HMC90 771; *HMC40 771*.

Lionel Rogg. *Complete Organ Works (1)*. Harmonia Mundi HMX290 772/83(1).

Lionel Rogg. *Complete Organ Works (2)*. Harmonia Mundi HMX290 772/83(2).

Lionel Rogg. *Complete Organ Works (3)*. Harmonia Mundi HMX290 772/83(3).

Wolfgang Rübsam (organ of Frauenfeld, Switzerland). Philips 420 860-2; *420 860-4*.

David Sanger (organ of St Catherine's College, Cambridge). Meridian ECD 84081.

David Sanger (organ of Kingston Parish Church). *Organ Works Volume 4*. Meridian CDE 84209.

Herbert Tachezi. Teldec 9031-74780-2; *9031-74780-4*.

Helmut Walcha (organ of St Laurentskerk, Alkmaar, Holland). Deutsche Grammophon 419 047-2; *419 047-4*.

Helmut Walcha (organ of St Laurentskerk, Alkmaar, Holland). Deutsche Grammophon *419 659-4*.

Helmut Walcha (organ of St Laurentskerk, Alkmaar, Holland). Deutsche Grammophon 427 191-2.

Bairstow, Sir Edward. Francis Jackson. Mirabilis MRCD 902; *MRC 902*.

Brahms, Johannes. Nicholas Danby. Continental Record Distributors CRD 3404;

Discography

CRDC 4104.

Dupré, Marcel. Jeremy Filsell (organ of Ely Cathedral). Gamut GAMCD530.

Daniel Roth. Motette CD10981.

Franck, César. Jennifer Bate. Unicorn DKPCD 9013; *DKPC 9013.*

Jennifer Bate. Unicorn Digital DKPCD 9014; *DKPC 9014.*

Jennifer Bate. Unicorn Digital DKPCD 9030; *DKPC 9030.*

François-Henri Houbart (Cavaillé-Coll organ of the Madeleine Church, Paris). Pierre Verany PV785031.

Peter Hurford. Argo Digital 411 710-2.

Michael Murray (organ of Symphony Hall, San Francisco, USA). Telarc Digital CD 80096.

Daniel Roth. *Organ Works Volume 1.* Motette CD11381.

Daniel Roth. *Organ Works Volume 2.* Motette CD11391.

Daniel Roth. *Organ Works Volume 3.* Motette CD11401.

Howells, Herbert. Christopher Dearnley. Hyperion Digital CDA 66260; *KA66260.*

Christopher Dearnley. Hyperion CDA 66394; *KA66394.*

Philip Kenyon. Herald HAVPCD115; *HAVPC 115.*

Langlais, Jean. O'Donnell/A. Lumsden. Hyperion Digital CDA 66270; *KA 66270.*

Lefébure-Wely, Louis. Jane Parker-Smith (Förster and Nicolaus organ in St Nikolaus, Frankfurt-am-Main). Motette CD 11691.

Liszt, Franz. Francesco Finotti (organ of the Tonhalle, Zürich). Edelweiss ED 1032.

Pierre Bousseau. *Organ Works.* ADDA 581030.

Pierre Bousseau. *Late Organ Works.* ADDA 581089.

David Sanger. Meridian CDE84060; *KE77060.*

Lorentzen, Bent. Frode Stengaard (organ of Aarhus Cathedral). Marco Polo/Da Capo DCCD 9009.

Mendelssohn, Felix. Peter Planyavsky. *Organ Works Volume 1.* Motette CD11271.

Peter Planyavsky. *Organ Works Volume 2.* Motette CD11281.

Peter Planyavsky. *Organ Works Volume 3.* Motette CD11291.

Messiaen, Olivier. Susan Landale. ADDA 581039.

Marie-Claire Alain. Erato 2292-45470-2.

Jennifer Bate. Unicorn DKPCD9024/5; *DKPC9024/5.*

Jennifer Bate. Unicorn DKPCD9028; *DKPC9028.*

Kevin Bowyer. Continuum CCD1011.

Mozart, Wolfgang Amadeus. Leo van Doeselaar. Globe GLO5063.

Poulenc, Francis. Zamkochian/Munch. RCA RD85750.

Saint-Saëns, Camille. Margaret Phillips. York CD110; *MC110.*

Peter Planyavsky. Motette CD11001.

Schumann, Robert. Thierry Mechler. Motette CD11041.

Vierne, Louis. Jennifer Bate (organ of Beauvais Cathedral, France). Unicorn Digital DKPCD9064; *DKPC9064.*

Daniel Roth. Motette CD10491.

The Organ

Widor, Charles-Marie. Peter Hurford (organ of Ratzeburg Cathedral, Germany). Argo Digital 410 165-2.
Thomas Trotter (organ of St François-de-Sales, Lyons). Argo 4331522.

Instrument recitals

Andrews, Colin. *Great European Organs No. 14* (organ of Bordeaux Cathedral, France). Priory PRCD 272.

Baker, David. *Baker's Dozen* (organ of Wymondham Abbey, Norfolk). Available from Wymondham Abbey Shop.
  Toccata from Wymondham (organ of Wymondham Abbey, Norfolk). Available from Wymondham Abbey Shop.

Barber, Graham. *Christmas Organ Music* (Schulze organ, Armley Parish Church, Leeds). Priory *PRC 232*.
  Great European Organs No. 8 (Klais organ of Ingoldstadt Minster, Germany). Priory Digital PRCD 260.
  Great European Organs No. 13 (Schulze organ at St Bartholomew's Church, Armley, Leeds). Priory Digital PRCD 269.
  Great European Organs No. 20 (organ of St Johannes Church, Osnabruck, Germany). Priory Digital PRCD 297.
  Great European Organs No. 23. Priory Digital PRCD 314.
  Great European Organs No. 25. Priory Digital PRCD 373.
  Great European Organs No. 27. Priory Digital PRCD 391.
  Dupré & Demessieux: Organ Works. Priory Digital PRCD 260.

Bate, Jennifer. *Two Centuries of British Organ Music* (organ of St James' Church, Muswell Hill, London). Hyperion Digital CDA 66180; *KA66180.*
  Virtuoso French Organ Music (organ of Beauvais Cathedral, France). Unicorn Digital DKPCD 99041; *DKPC 9041.*

Bielby, Jonathan. *Great European Organs No. 21* (Binns organ of Rochdale Town Hall). Priory PRCD 298.

Briggs, David. *Great European Organs No. 16* (Father Willis organ of St George's Hall, Liverpool). Priory PRCD 284.

Britton, Harold. *Organ Spectacular* (organ of the Royal Albert Hall). ASV CDQS 6028.

Cleobury, Stephen. *British Organ Music from King's* (organ of King's College, Cambridge). Priory *PRC 169.*
  Great European Organs No.1 (organ of King's College, Cambridge). Priory Digital PRCD 185; *PRC 185.*

Curley, Carlo. *The Emperor's Fanfare* (organ of Girard College Chapel, Philadelphia). Argo Digital 430 200-2; *430 200-4.*
  Brightly Shining – Romantic Organ Music. Argo 430 837-2ZH; *430 837-4ZH.*
  Organ Imperial – Works by British Composers. Argo 433 450-2ZH; *433 4540-4ZH.*
  The Organ's Greatest Hits. RCA GD 90533; *GK 90533.*

Derrett, Paul. *Complete Organ Works of Henri Mulet* (organ of Notre Dame de Grace,

Discography

Leicester Square, London). Priory Digital PRCD 242 AB (Double).

Filsell, Jeremy. *French Organ Works*. Herald HAVPCD 145.

20th Century English Organ Music. Gamut GAMCD 524.

Herrick, Christopher. *The Guilmant Organ Sonatas, Volume 1* (organ of Katwijk aan Zee, Holland). Priory PRC 230.

Organ Fireworks (organ of Westminster Abbey). Hyperion CDA 66121; *KA 66121*.

Organ Fireworks IV (organ of St Bartholomew's Church, New York). Hyperion CDA 66605.

Hill, David. *Organ Spectacular* (organ of Westminster Cathedral). Pickwick Digital PCD 823.

Hurford, Peter. *Baroque Organ Music* (organ of Bethlehemkerk, Papendrecht, Holland). Argo 414 496-2.

Romantic Organ Music (organ of Ratzeburg Cathedral, Germany). Argo Digital 410 165-2.

Great Organ Works (organ of Sydney Opera House). Decca Digital 425 013-2DM; *425 013-4DM*.

John, Keith. *Bach & Reubke* (Kleuker organ of the Tonhalle, Zürich, Switzerland). Priory Digital PRCD 264.

Great European Organs No. 2 (organ of l'Eglise du Chant d'Oiseau, Brussels, Belgium). Priory Digital PRCD 174; *PRC 174*.

Great European Organs No. 6 (organ of l'Eglise Notre Dame des Neiges à l'Alpe d'Huez, France). Priory Digital PRCD 235.

Lancelot, James. *Great European Organs No. 5* (organ of Durham Cathedral). Priory Digital PRCD 228; *PRC 228*.

Lucas, Adrian. *Romantic Organ Frolics* (organs of Norwich Cathedral and St Andrew's Hall, Norwich). Priory *PRC 180*.

Marshall, Kimberley. *Great European Organs No. 11* (Cavaillé-Coll organ of St Sernin, Toulouse, France). Priory Digital PRCD 261.

Organ Works (organ of Littlefield House, Portola Valley, California). IMP Classics PCD 1005.

Millington, Andrew. *The Versatile English Organ* (organ of Wymondham Abbey). Priory Digital PRCD 268.

Parker-Smith, Jane. *Popular French Romantics Volume 1* (organ of Coventry Cathedral). ASV Digital CDDCA 539; *ZCDCA 539*.

Popular French Romantics Volume 2 (organ of Beauvais Cathedral). ASV Digital CDDCA 610; *ZCDCA 610*.

Payne, Joseph. *Early English Organ Music Volume 1*. Naxos 8 550718.

Early English Organ Music Volume 2. Naxos 8 550719.

Phillips, Margaret. *18th Century English Organ Music* (organ of St Matthew's Church, Westminster). Gamut GAMCD 514.

Preston, Simon. *The World of the Organ*. Decca 430 091-2DWO; *430 091-4DWO*.

Rees-Williams, Jonathan. *Organ Music from Windsor Castle* (organ of St George's Hall).

Heritage HRCD 921.

The Organ of Lichfield Cathedral. Abbey CDCA 902; *CACA 902*.

Romanov, Boris. *Organ Music in Moscow* (organ of the Great Hall at the Moscow Conservatory). Harmonia Mundi CDMLDC288 020.

Scott, John. *Mathias – Organ Works* (organ of St Paul's Cathedral, London). Nimbus NI 5367.

Scott Whiteley, John. *Great European Organs No. 12* (organ of St Bavo's Church, Haarlem, Holland). Priory Digital PRCD 265.

Great Romantic Organ Music (organ of York Minster). York CD 101; *MC 101*.

Favourite Organ Works (organ of St Paul's Cathedral). Cirrus CICD 1007.

Trepte, Paul. *Organ Music from Northern Europe* (organ of Ely Cathedral). Gamut GAMCD 532.

Walsh, Colin. *French Organ Music* (organ of Salisbury Cathedral). Priory *PRC 148*.

Great European Organs No. 15 (organ of Lincoln Cathedral). Priory Digital PRCD 281; *PRC 281*.

French Organ Music. Priory Digital PRCD 905.

Watts, Jane. *Great European Organs No. 7* (organ of Westminster Abbey). Priory Digital PRCD 237.

Great European Organs No. 18 (organ of Chartres Cathedral, France). Priory Digital PRCD 286.

Great European Organs No. 19 (Cavaillé-Coll organ of Orléans Cathedral, France) Priory Digital PRCD 294.

Wills, Arthur. *Great European Organs No. 9* (organ of Ely Cathedral). Priory Digital PRCD 246.

Index

Compiled by Joan Welsby

Note that the index covers only the main text and not the gazetteer, bibliography or discography. Italicised page numbers denote an illustration.

Action: electric 9-10, 12, 15, 17, 51-2
electro-pneumatic 9, 12, 15, 17, 51
mechanical 9, 15
tracker 9-10, 17, 25, 56
tubular-pneumatic 9-10, 12, 15, 51
Adlington Hall *35*, 38, 53
Alain, J. 75
Albert Hall, London 49
Alkmaar, St Laurents *27*, 29, 30
Amsterdam, Oude Kerk 69
Andely, Le Petit, Rouen *34*
Anglican Church, organ in 8
Antiphonal use of organ 34
Aquincum, Hungary 19
Armley, St Bartholomew 51, *54*, *55*
Arnaut, H. 24
Arrangements, musical. *See* Preludes, chorale
Ashton-under-Lyne, St Michael *45*
Bach, J. S. 49, 56, 59, 62, *66*, *67*, 68, 70-4
Bamboo 6
Barker, C. S. 51
Barking, All Hallows 37
Barrel organ 56, 76
Bassoon (organ stop) 5, 15, 47
Beethoven, L. van 47, 73
Belfast, Ulster Hall 49
Bellows 5, 8, 19, 60
hand-pumped 23-4
number in early organ 20
Benedictine order:
interest in music 20
use of organ allowed 19, 37
Berlioz, H. 47
Bird whistles (organ stops) 49, 52
Birmingham Town Hall 46, 49
Bishop, J. C. 51
Blackpool, Tower Ballroom 53
Block Flute 13-14
Blockwerk 26
Blow, J. 73

Blowing mechanism 8, 10, *71*
Böhm, G. 71
Bolton Town Hall *41*
Bombarde 11, 32, 62
Boot, of reed pipe 5
Bordeaux Cathedral *31*
Boston, Music Hall 51
Bourdon 14, 16
Boyce, W. 73
Brahms, J. 74, *75*
Britain 11, 13, 19, 34-5, 37-8, 40-2, 49, 51, 53, 56, 57, 65, 68-9, 72-3, 76
Britten, B. 76
Bruhns, N. 71
Brüstwerk 29
Bull, J. 69
Buxtehude, D. 70
Carisbrooke Castle 53, *54*
Case, organ 12-13, 17, 30, 32, 38, 42, 51, 61
Catholic Church, organ in 37, 65, 69
Cavaillé-Coll, A. 47, 49, 51, 57, 63, 75
Chaconne 66, 70
Chair, organ division 11, 24, 38, 41
Chalfont Heights, house organ *57*
Chamber music 71
Chamber organ 11, 53-4
Chelsea, St John *56*
Chichester Cathedral *50*
Chimney Flute 14
Choir: manual 13, 15, 45
organ division 11, 14, 16, 38, 41, 47
singing 21, 34, 65
Chorale 65-6, 70-1, 74-5
Chorus stops 11, 13, 16, 26, 32, 34, 37, 49, 54, 61-3
Cinema organ 52-3, 76
Clarion 13-15, 47, 63
Clavierübung (J. S. Bach) 71, 73
Clerambault, L. N. 72
Clerkenwell: St James *39*
St Peter's Italian church *42*
Compton, J. 53
Concerto 68, 71, 73, 76
Cone, tuning 7, 13
Console 10, 29
Continuo, organ as 54

Conveyancing tubes 34, 61
Cornet (organ stop) 14, 16, 25, 34, 41, 46-7, 54, 62, 73
Couperin, F. *63*, 72
Coupler 13-14, 17, 42, 45, 61
Coupling manuals 11, 16, 24, 32, 51, 60, 62-4
Croft, W. 73
Crumhorn (Krummhorn) 25
Cymbale (Cymbel, Cimbel) (mixture stop) 14, 32
Cymbals (organ stop) 49
Cymbel 14, 16
Cymbelstern 25, 49
Dallam, T. 55
D'Andrieu, J. F. 72
Diapason 13-14, 16, 38, 47, 61-3, 73
Dixon, R. 53
Doncaster Parish Church 51
Duddington, A. 37
Dulciana 13-14
Dynamics 11, 60, 64
Echo: effect 34
'Fantasia' (Sweelinck) 69
organ manual 11, 32, 41, 63
Elgar, E. 76
Ely Cathedral 57
En chamade 13, 34
Fairground organ 56, 76
Fanfare: battle 13
great occasion 21
Fantasia 67, 70-1, *75*. *See also* Echo
Fugue on BACH (Liszt) 74
Fifteenth (organ stop) 13-16, 47, 63
Flageolet 14, 16
Flue pipes 5-7, *7*, 8, 30-1, 35, 61-2
Flute: instrument 5
organ stop 14, 16, 25, 34, 47, 51, 53, 62-3
Foghorns (special effect) 52
Fourniture (basic mixture stop) 32, 47
France 13, 15-16, 19, 31-2,

34, 38, 40-1, 47, 49, 57, 62-3, 65, 72, 75-6
Franck, C. 49, 75
Freiberg Cathedral 29, 31
Frescobaldi, G. 69
Frobenius, T. 56
Froberger, J. J. 69
Fugue 66-7, 71, 74-5
Furniture. *See* Fourniture 47
Gamba (organ stop) 49
Gauntlett, H. J. 49
Gedackt 14
Germany 16, 22, 25-6, 29, 30-2, 34, 38, 41, 47, 49, 51, 56, 64-5, 69-70, 74-6
Granada Cathedral 33
'Grand Jeu' 34, 62
Greene, M. 73
Grigny, N. de 72
Haarlem, St Bavo *28*, 29-30
Halberstadt Cathedral 22, *22*, 23
Halifax Parish Church 42, 45
Handel, G. F. 73
Harmonium 55, 69
Harpsichord 5, 59, 69, 71, 74
Harris, R. 40-1, 54
Harrison and Harrison 49, 51
Hauptwerk 26, 29, 31, 62
Hautboy 14, 46
Haydn, F. J. 56, 73
Herschel, W. 46
Hill, W. 49
Hohlflute 14, 16
Holborn, St Andrew *82*
Holywell Music Room *21*
Hope-Jones, R. 52
Horizontal pipes 13, 34
Horn (organ stop), Basset 14, 16
Horsforth, Our Lady of Good Counsel *48*
Hydraulis and *cornu* players 20
Hydraulos 19
Hymn 12, 26, 65, 68, 69, 71, 73
Improvising 65, 67-8, 73, 75
Italy 34-5, 38, 57, 66, 69
Jongen, J. 75
Jordan, A. 41

Karg-Elert, S. 75
Kinura 53
Krebs, J. L. 71
Ktesibios 19
Lancing College Chapel 43
Langlais, J. 75
Languid (organ pipe) 8
Larigot 14, 16
Liszt, F. 47, 74, *74*
Liverpool, Anglican Cathedral 8, *8*
Lübeck, V. 71
Lugge, J. 38
Magdalen College, Oxford *4*, 38
Magnet, in electric action 10
Mass: Catholic 37, 65
   organ 65, 72, 75
   plainsong 71
Medieval organ 14, 19, 21-3, 37, 53, 64
Mendelssohn, F. 73
Messiaen, O. 75-6
Microchips 55
Mixture stop 10, 13-14, 16, 22, 31-2, 37, 41, 46, 63
Monasteries 21, 47, 72
Montre 32
Mouth 5
Mozart, W. A. 56, 73
Müller, C. 30
Mutation stops 13, 25, 30, 34, 41, 49, 61-2
Nag's Head Swell mechanism 42, *42*, 46
Nave organ 12
Nazard 25
Neo-classical organ 56
New Jersey 51
Nicks (in pipe metal) 8
Nineteenth (organ stop) 63
Notes inégales 63, 72
Oberwerk 29
Oboe 5, 14, 46. *See also* Hautboy
Octave (organ stop) 14, 16
Old Radnor, St Stephen 38
Ophicleide 14-15
Organ: accompanimental instrument 19, 21, 37, 52-3, 55, 76
   general section *17*
   under construction *58*
Organo ad libitum 73
Organo pleno 62
Orgelbüchlein (J. S. Bach) 71
Orgue, Grande 32, 34, 62
Oriel College, Oxford *38*
Orthodox Church 19

Ottobeuren Abbey, Bavaria *32, 34*
Pachelbel, J. 71
Paisley Abbey *84*
Pallet, in organ mechanism 9, 56, 59
Pan-pipes 19
Paris: St Clothilde 49
   St Sulpice Basilica 49
Partita 65
Passacaglia 65
Pedal 9, 11, 22, 25, 30, 32, 35, 37-8, 51, 53, 59, 64, 66, 72, 75
   board 16, 22, 74
   combination 60
   division 11, 13, 16-17, 29-30, 32, 34, 41, 49, 61
   harpsichord 74
   organ 14
   piano 74
   pull-downs 40-1
   solos 63
   See also Swell
Pembroke College, Cambridge *36*
Pepin, King 19
Percussion (stops) 49
'Petit Plein Jeu' 62
Piano 1, 59-60, 73-4
Pipe 6-16, 19, 22-3, 25, 35, 45, 53, 55, 59, 73
   conical 5
   foot 5
   mouth 5
   principal 5
Piston 12, 14, 17, 51, 64
Pitch 5-7, 10, 12-14, 16, 24, 32, 34, 53, 61, 63
Plainchant 21, 66, 69, 71
   melodies 65
   singing of 26, 64
'Plein Jeu' 34, 62
Portative organ 23
Positive *18, 23*, 23, 24, 26, 31-2, 34, 62
   and Regal 25
Praetorius, M. 69
Prelude 65, 67, 71, 73
   chorale 65, 70-1, 73, 75
Principal: pipes 47, 51, 54, 61-3
   stops 5, 11, 13-14, 16, 29-30, 34
Pulsator organorum 19
Purcell, H. 73
Queen's College, Oxford 56
Recit (organ division) 32, 41
Reed: pedal 62
   pipes 5, 8, 24
   rank 32, 49, 54
   stops 8, 13-16, 23, 25, 34-5, 38, 41, 61-3, 72

Regal 24, 38, 53
Reger, M. 75
Registration: aids 12, 17, 51, 60-1, 64
   art of 59, 63
   stop 11-13, 15, 17, 26, 30, 34, 37, 47, 53, 60-5, 72
Repertoire 64
   church music 65
   classical 49, 69
   organist's 70-1, 74-5
Reubke, J. 74
Rheinberger, J. 75
Robertsbridge Codex 22
Royal Scottish Academy *40*
Rückpositiv 26, *26*, 30-1
Sackbut 14, 25
St Albans International Organ Festival organ *57*
'St Anne' Fugue 71
St Mary-at-Hill church 49
St Paul's Cathedral 5, 41, 73
Salicional 14, 16
Salisbury Cathedral 40
Scheidt, S. 69
Schlick, A. 25
Schnitger, F. C. 29, 31
Schübler Chorale Preludes (J. S. Bach) 71
Schultze family 51, 54
Schumann, R. 74
Sesquialtera 46-7
Seventeenth (organ stop) 13-14, 16, 62
Shawm 14
Shostakovich, D. 76
Silbermann family 31, 51
Sion, Notre Dame de Valère 23, *24*
Slider 10, 17, 19-20, 22, 25
Smith, B. 40-1, 54, 78
Snetzler, J. 42, 54
Solo: division 11
   effects 32, 34
   melody 25, 61
   organ as solo instrument 64-5, 68, 76
   pedal 66
   registers 47
   stops 13, 16, 25, 30-1, 34, 49, 53-4, 62-3, 73
Sonata 67, 73-5
Southwick, St James Without the Priory Gates *40*
Stanley, J. 72, 73
Stockholm: National Historical Museum 23
Stopper in pipe 5, 16

Sweelinck, J. P. *68*, 69, *70*
Swell: box 11, 47, 60
   division 16-17, 35, 42, 49, 60
   manual 11, 16, 63
   organ 14, 47
   pedal 11
   shutters 41
   stops 16
Symphony 68, 75
Syrinx 19
Thursford *52*, 53
Tibia 53
Tierce 25, 46
en taille 34
Tin, as pipe material 6
Tippett, M. 76
Titelouze, J. 69
Toccata 66, 69, 71, 75
Tournemire, C. 75
Tremulant 14, 16, 25, 53
Trinity College, Dublin *44*
Trio Sonata 59, 61, 68, 71
Trombone 14
Trumpet (organ stop) 13-15, 25, 47, 62-3, 73
Tuning 7-8, 16
Turkey, Sultan of 19, 55
Twelfth (organ stop) 13-14, 47, 63
United States of America 46-7, 51, 53, 55, 57, 76
Ventil 64
Viola da Gamba (organ stop) 14-16
Vivaldi, A. 71
Voix Celeste 14, 16, 49
Voluntary 38, 68, 73
Vox Humana 47, 63
Wagner, R. 68
Walcker of Ludwigsburg 51
Walond, W. 73
Walther, J. G. 71
Weingarten Abbey, Bavaria *30*, 31
Werkprinzip organ 26, 29-31, 47, 56, 60, 62
Westminster Abbey 37, 73
Widor, C. M. 49, 75
Willis, H. 49, 51
Winchester Cathedral, 20, 37
Windchest 5, 8-11, 19, 22-3, 25, 34, 37, 56, 60-1, 64
Worcester Cathedral 53
Wren, Sir Christopher 5
Wurlitzer organ 53
Wymondham Abbey 2, *6, 9, 10, 12, 14, 15, 16-17*
Zinc, as pipe material 6